Electing Madam Vice President

Communicating Gender

Series Editors: Diana Bartelli Carlin, Saint Louis University, Nichola D. Gutgold, Pennsylvania State University, and Theodore F. Sheckels, Randolph-Macon College

Communicating Gender features original research examining the role gender plays in communication. It encompasses a wide variety of approaches and methodologies to explore theoretically relevant topics pertaining to the interrelation of gender and communication both in the United States and worldwide. This series examines gender issues broadly, ranging from masculine hegemony and gender issues in political culture to media portrayals of women and men and the work/life balance.

Recent Titles in This Series

Electing Madam Vice President: When Women Run Women Win, by Nichola D. Gutgold
Communicating Intimate Health, edited by Angela Cooke-Jackson and Valerie Rubinsky
Misogyny across Global Media, edited by Maria B. Marron
Reimagining Black Masculinities: Race, Gender, and Public Space, edited by Mark C. Hopson and Mika'il Petin
Intersectionality: Understanding Women's Lives and Resistance, edited by Dawn L. Hutchinson and Lori Underwood
Misogyny and Media in the Age of Trump, edited by Maria B. Marron
The Rhetorical Arts of Women in Aviation, 1911-1970: Name It and Take It, by Sara Hillin
Food Blogs, Postfeminism, and the Construction of Expertise: Digital Domestics, by Alane Presswood
Developing Women Leaders in the Academy through Enhanced Communication Strategies, edited by Jayne Cubbage
Empowering Women: Global Voices of Rhetorical Influence, by Julia Spiker
Technofeminist Storiographies: Women, Information Technology, and Cultural Representation, by Kristine Blair
Women of the 2016 Election: Voices, Views, and Values, edited by Jennifer Schenk Sacco

Electing Madam Vice President

When Women Run Women Win

Nichola D. Gutgold

Foreword by Loretta T. Avent
Afterword by Congresswoman Susan Wild

LEXINGTON BOOKS
Lanham • Boulder • New York • London

Published by Lexington Books
An imprint of The Rowman & Littlefield Publishing Group, Inc.
4501 Forbes Boulevard, Suite 200, Lanham, Maryland 20706
www.rowman.com

6 Tinworth Street, London SE11 5AL, United Kingdom

British Library Cataloguing in Publication Information Available

Library of Congress Cataloging-in-Publication Data

Library of Congress Control Number: 2021933345

ISBN 978-1-7936-2219-8 (cloth)
ISBN 978-1-7936-2221-1 (pbk)
ISBN 978-1-7936-2220-4 (electronic)

This book is dedicated to all the women who ever dared to lead.
Whether it be in politics, at a school board
meeting, or even in her own home.
Thank you for making the world a more equal place.

An Ode to the 2020 Election
Six women were in the race,
The first "presidential" debate was a total disgrace,
What would be this country's ace?
A president with a woman's face!

Nichola D. Gutgold 2020

Contents

A Foreword in Verse

by Loretta T. Avent

It was a rainy and warm July evening in Philadelphia, Pennsylvania, in 2016 when Nichola Gutgold and I met for the first time. They say that some things are just meant to happen, and this chance meeting at the Democratic National Convention on the evening of Hillary Clinton's acceptance of the Democratic nomination for president was one of those things. There was a long evening ahead of us and we did what most strangers do; we took up some small talk. I learned that she was a college professor with a twenty-plus-year history of writing about women in nontraditional fields. We were quickly deep into conversation when my cell phone rang and Wayne called for me to come to my front row seat with the rest of the Hillaryland team so we would be in a position to immediately join her on stage after her acceptance speech. My beloved granddaughter Brittany might have regretted that missed historical opportunity for her because Hillary had played a very important role in her life. Something inside me told me that I was sitting (way up high in the non-VIP seats) exactly where I was supposed to be. Nichola, since that day, played a significant role in Brittany's life, too, as they are about to coauthor their third children's book together. When I worked as the deputy assistant to the President for Intergovernmental Affairs, White House Liaison to Indian Country and Liaison to the First Lady's Office in the Clinton White House, I saw up close many of the issues that Dr. Gutgold researches and writes about. Working in Hillaryland (as we affectionately called it) I also had a front row seat to history, as have the women in this book in their quests to achieve political offices at every level, but especially the office of the U.S. presidency.

I could write a traditional foreword that underscores what is in the book, but that would be traditional, and this book is all about new traditions.

Be assured that this carefully researched and well-written book preserves the presidential bids of six women who dared to put themselves into the presidential arena and is worth your time and attention to read. This book represents progress yes, but like most daring achievements, there's more to address.

This book details six women for President
Natural-born citizen, 35 and 14 year resident
Now girls can believe
that Madam President is theirs to achieve
Little girls who for too many years
Muted their dreams because of fears
Remember, too that the first Americans who made America we all share
Deserve their own recognition as they and their little girls prepare
To go from Tribal women leaders to thinking about actually being
The leader of the free world and their little girls are now seeing
We owe many Native American women and her beloved people a debt
That still remains open but that payment will be made yet
R.I.P. Shirley Chisholm and thank you for opening the door
Where in America no other African American woman dared attempt before
As this book's author has been writing about for so many years
Paving the way for Madam President is now near enough for cheers
To be toasted because chosen in 2020 was Madam Vice President
We are now closer than ever to the final breaking of the glass ceiling's intent
That women have forced to be broken forever and the barriers of yesterday
Are disappearing as Vice President Harris is now onward forward on the paved way.

Loretta T. Avent was deputy assistant to the President for Intergovernmental Affairs, White House Liaison to Indian Country and Liaison to First Lady's Office in the Clinton White House. She is an advocate for Grand families and Native Americans.

Acknowledgments

Several people helped me get this book into your hands, and I am grateful. Brittany Avent of Arizona State University was an enthusiastic research assistant, who brought younger generation insight into the project as did my former Penn State student, Fatima Alba, who shot and styled the photo of the political buttons on the front cover. Special thanks to Nicolette Amstutz at Lexington Books whom I have enjoyed working with for several years and who always responds to ideas with support and encouragement. Alan Janesch, a top-notch editor, was easy and pleasant to work with, spent his time and considerable talent making the manuscript better. Loretta T. Avent, who wrote the foreword for this book, is an incredible person whose insights into politics and life make not only the foreword of this book valuable, but as a mentor to me, has increased the meaning and joy in my life as well. To my Pen Is Mightier writing club friends, thanks for listening to early versions of the introductory chapter. To Congresswoman Susan Wild not only for her astute afterword but for her service to my Pennsylvania district and our country. She is a true trailblazer who leads with both her heart and her head. And always, to my husband Geoff, who supplies the world's best coffee and a steady stream of newspaper articles, nonstop love, and encouragement. To our adult children Ian and Emi who have grown up listening to the latest book project idea come to life. Thank you all!

Introduction

The Changing Rhetoric of Women and Presidential Politics

It was July 2016, at the Democratic National Convention, in the uppermost section of seats in the massive Wells Fargo Center, Philadelphia. A mother and father and their two young girls—maybe five and six years old—were waiting. Waiting for the woman who could become the next president of the United States to take the stage and share her vision for the country. The electricity in the air was palpable.

From my coveted seat in the convention hall, watching the family in the row directly in front of mine, I couldn't help thinking of the family outings I had taken part in as a child: visits to the beach, walks in the woods, and days at a small, family-run amusement park near my childhood home. What I was witnessing before me was a family outing not unlike those of my youth, except this one had a history lesson built in. The family in front of me was waiting not for a carnival, or a dip in the ocean, but for Hillary Clinton to accept the Democratic Party's nomination for president.

As for myself, I did not have a seat at the convention because I have political connections. Far from it. But as a university professor in the field of communication arts and sciences, I have been studying women and the American presidency for two decades. That summer, I was working as a faculty member for a nonprofit educational organization that offers college students a chance to experience the unique rhetorical artifact that is a political convention. I was in the convention hall only because a remarkably kind professor who had a ticket knew of my long-standing research interest and graciously allowed me to use his pass into the convention hall.

I felt especially thrilled to be there at this particularly important moment. As one by one the speakers emerged, spoke, and then left the stage, the tiny, ponytailed girls in the row in front of me started to get sleepy. As they began to curl up in the fetal position—their small bodies huddled onto the uncomfortable plastic arena seats—the large, vertical, blue-and-white "Stronger, Together" placards they had been clutching at the beginning of the evening started to tip over and fall into their laps and behind their seats.

It was late in the evening, way past their bedtimes. But now it was *time*. Their parents nudged them awake, as a woman clad in a white pantsuit—the Democratic nominee for president, Hillary Clinton—took to the stage as a Rachel Platten's "Fight Song" pulsated through the cavernous stadium. "Can you hear my voice? This time this is my fight song. . . . My power's turned on. . . . I've still got a lot of fight left in me!" The words and music faded as Hillary Clinton's voice began her historic speech.

Declaring that the nation was at "a moment of reckoning," Clinton urged voters to reject Donald J. Trump's divisive policies and combative politics. As the *New York Times* put it, Clinton "offered herself as a steady and patriotic American who would stand up for citizens of all races and creeds and unite the country to persevere against Islamic terrorists, economic troubles, and the chaos of gun violence."[1]

As the two little girls in front of me watched intently, I could not help wondering what they were thinking. For me, this outing was more thrilling than any day at an amusement park. What I was witnessing, I thought, was the first woman president in U.S. history. I found myself wishing my mom could be there with me. And in a way, I felt as though she *was* there—as were the hopes and dreams of many women past and present who dared to go where no woman had gone before. As we know, the election turned out differently. The prize that American women had dreamed about for generations did not go to one of their own.

And yet, the lessons from 2016 and other women who have blazed trails remain highly instructive. Hillary Clinton's bids for the presidency in both 2008 and 2016 represented the first times in U.S. history that a woman was not a symbolic presidential candidate. In 2008, Clinton came close to clinching the Democratic nomination ultimately won by Barack Obama. In 2016, Clinton won the Democratic nomination for president. We know this history, but do we know where it has led us? Since that electrifying evening in Philadelphia, and the historic 2018 midterm election, where does America stand on the subject of women and the presidency? Does 2016 mean anything to women's political future? And what in the world, if anything, does "electability" have to do with it? *Is* there a desire on the part of a majority of Americans to elect a woman president? If so, why? Is it just because we have not had one? Is that a good enough reason? Or is it about equality and inclusion? Will a woman president change America?

These are all questions that need a larger sample than one to answer. And while we don't yet even have one to sample—while not even one woman candidate has ever attained the office of president—all these questions inform the content of this book, which examines the presidential bids of six women in 2020 and focuses on the gender implications of their races.

The greatest advantages any politician can have as a presidential candidate are to gain the national spotlight early in the primary season and stay there—garnering media attention, using all the tools of a campaign to get voters to know them, and ultimately securing their votes.

Historically, relative to the number of male candidates, so few women have run for president of the United States that they were either forgotten about in the press and in the public's mind or regarded as merely symbolic candidates with no chance of winning. As a rule, they were not considered or even mentioned as legitimate contenders. Many of the women candidates for president in past elections are not even discussed in most history books, not even in the footnotes. (We now call these kinds of slights microaggressions.)

For decades it seemed that women could not be seen as presidential material, even if, indeed, they ran for president. For example, in his 2000 book, *Hats in the Ring*, Brad Koplinski interviews twenty-eight presidential candidates, only two of whom are women (Shirley Chisholm and Patsy Mink, both from 1972 election). And yet he includes such unknown or little-known men such as Larry Agran and Reubin Askew. Eleanor Clift and Tom Brazaitis, in *Madam President: Shattering the Last Glass Ceiling*, a groundbreaking book from the same year, put gender constraints this way: "Candidates in the end are judged by the picture they paint of themselves and overcoming gender bias is like dealing with any other disadvantage going into a competitive race."[2] In other words, being female just puts another obstacle on the path to the presidency.

This book is a rhetorical study of the six women who have run for president. In it, I seek to discover whether Hillary Clinton's history-making nomination in 2016 and the subsequent largest-ever number of women who ran for the Democratic nomination (at one time) in 2020 have changed the rhetoric of presidential politics. If there was ever a year in presidential politics when gender did a full 360-degree turn, 2016 in the United States would seem to be it. Yes, a woman did garner the Democratic nomination for president, the very first woman in U.S. history to do so, but she lost to Donald Trump, a businessman with no experience whatsoever in electoral politics. Trump's view of women and how to win in American politics took the United States on a coarse path where no one—especially women—was immune to ridicule in the name of winning. Trump's visceral disdain for his opponent, Hillary Clinton, was palpable; he stopped at nothing to portray her as an old, corrupt woman, shamelessly chanting "Lock Her Up!"[3] along with his rally-goers. As Kelly L. Winfrey and James M. Schnoebelen succinctly wrote in a journal article on gender and political communications, "No office has proven more challenging for women candidates than the U.S. Presidency. Heading into

Election Day 2016 many believed the U.S. would elect its first female president, Hillary Clinton, and were shocked as results poured in and news outlets began calling the election for political novice Donald Trump."[4] Although Donald Trump's victory was surprising to many, 2016 was an important marker for women and U.S. presidential politics.

Before Hillary Clinton won the Democratic nomination, only two other women—Geraldine Ferraro in 1984 and Sarah Palin in 2008—had made it to a national political ticket, and both were vice presidential candidates. The fact that Hillary Clinton had won more votes seemed irrelevant in a country in which the Electoral College decides the winner. It was a tough loss for many. (Among those feeling that loss, no doubt, was the family sitting in front of me at the Democratic National Convention. It seemed that the parents had come to see the first woman president and had brought their two young daughters along to witness the history for themselves. Perhaps, the parents hoped, their daughters would someday tell their own grandchildren how they were there when the first woman president in the United States accepted the nomination.) As this book also chronicles, a third woman would make it into the vice presidential arena as a result of the 2020 election—California senator Kamala Harris. Her own bid for the presidency in the primary in 2020 likely had everything to do with why former vice president Joseph R. Biden Jr. chose her as his running mate.

WHAT DOES IDENTITY HAVE TO DO
WITH PRESIDENTIAL POLITICS?

Maybe you have heard this question before: Why does the gender identity of our president matter? Because academic research, including my own, has revealed that having a diversity of people in elected office widens the aperture of possibilities. In seminal research on gender and politics, C. L. Bower argued that stereotypical perceptions of the identity of women candidates both hurt and help their political aspirations. While it is positive for both men and women to be seen as empathic and caring, that perception may also disadvantage women. Why? Because most voters, assuming that women will have these characteristics, may question whether a woman could be tough enough to handle the sometimes rough-and-tumble demands of political office.[5] Since we have not had a woman president, voters may look with a more discerning (and even critical) eye at women candidates. They may wonder if a woman can effectively lead, since leadership requires a candidate to be tough and decisive. Even women who interview politicians come under scrutiny. For example, NBC News correspondent Kristen Welker served as a much more effective debate moderator than Fox News anchor Chris Wallace during the

2020 election. While no one questioned in advance Wallace's ability to keep the candidates in line (as it turned out, he could not), news outlets seemed surprised that Welker had full command of the candidates in the second and final presidential debate.

With six women running for president in 2020, the country seemed to be inching toward the critical mass of candidates needed for women to gain political parity, as argued in early gender political research—although no precise number has ever been linked with that critical mass.[6] As Richard L. Fox noted in a 2011 study, researchers have made substantial strides in explaining the role of gender in U.S. politics. In terms of electoral politics, it has become clear that there is no widespread gender bias in general election outcomes. However, gender continues to exert significant influence on the way that women come to enter the political arena.[7] A woman running for political office is routinely described by the press and public as a "woman candidate." Yet there is no similar marker for male candidates, such as "male presidential candidate." This way of describing women candidates alone calls attention to identity. (I concede this entire study does as well.)

Examining the words and the communication styles of the six women who ran for the Democratic nomination for president in 2020 provides an opportunity to see how gender plays a role in the sharing of political issues and what rhetorical opportunities and obstacles may be inherent in that communication. For example, Amy Klobuchar notes that she was inspired to run for political office when she was sent home early from the hospital after giving birth to her daughter. Elizabeth Warren tells many stories of her mother's efforts to save the family and her own release from her job once it was revealed she was pregnant. Kirsten Gillibrand shares how her appearance has influenced how she is covered in the media, and Marianne Williamson asserts that being a woman influenced how her nonviolent message was received. How politicians frame the issues they talk about cannot help but reveal their own gendered experiences. While both male and female candidates discuss the same issues, such as health care, the economy, and education, how they talk about the issues is inextricably tied to their gendered experiences. An iconic photo of President John Kennedy in the Oval Office shows his toddler son, John Kennedy Jr., playing underneath his desk. If President Kennedy had been a woman, such a photo would no doubt have called attention to the lack of appropriate childcare or the distractions created by her child playing in her workspace.

With the increase of women candidates for political office at all levels, it seems that we are getting closer to answering the fundamental question that remains: When will a woman be elected president? A number of scholarly studies since the early 2000s have set out to answer that question. Many of these studies build on the scholarship of Linda Witt, Glenna Matthews, and

Karen M. Paget.[8] In their prescient 1994 book, *Running as a Woman: Gender and Power in American Politics*, they concluded that when we have a critical mass of women running for office, including the presidency of the United States, women will be more likely to gain political parity. Kristina Horn Sheeler and Karrin Vasby Anderson, in their 2013 book, *Woman President: Confronting Postfeminist Political Culture*, argue that media frames are partly responsible for sexualizing women candidates in the voter's eyes, and that fictional popular culture portrayals of women candidates and presidents help inch forward history. Erika Falk's *Women for President: Media Bias in Nine Campaigns* examines the press culture of women presidential candidates. Hillary Clinton's 2017 campaign postmortem, *What Happened*, also helps the public understand some of the candidate's perceptions of how her closest bid for the presidency eluded her. In the United States, a country heralded for democracy, why has political leadership been so skewed by gender? Why did it take so long to even get to the point where several women were running in one presidential race? We may not ever have a definitive answer to that question.

THE CONTRIBUTION OF THIS BOOK

This book offers a rhetorical analysis of the six women running for president in the 2020 presidential primary. Did the number of women running for president in 2020 allow them all to escape the sexist tropes of being "the woman" running? No, unfortunately it did not. However, it did allow them to be their authentic selves in ways that each chapter examines. It also showed that women can be viable candidates. Even though none rose to win the nomination, each made an individual case for their candidacy in a way that was true to herself, and more importantly, believable to some voters. The bid of Kamala Harris also likely put her on to the short list of possible vice presidential candidates once Joe Biden committed to choosing a woman.

Each chapter will offer an overview of the candidate's presidential race, and set the scene about each woman's presidential bid, from her announcement speech to her withdrawal from the race. It also places the 2020 contest into perspective, by offering a view of what was happening in presidential politics at time these women were making their presidential bids. Each chapter will present a brief biography of each candidate, followed by a neo-Aristotelian analysis of her invention, disposition, and memoria, as well as notable media coverage and the takeaways from her campaign. The final chapter offers an analysis of the eventual vice presidential pick, Kamala Harris, only the third woman ever in the United States to be on a national ticket as a vice presidential candidate. The concluding chapter aims to illuminate what was different about her campaign, thirty-six years after the first woman vice president, Geraldine Ferraro, was on the ticket with Walter Mondale.

Because none of the women in this book won the presidency, their bids as presidential hopefuls would likely end up forgotten if not documented and examined for their unique rhetorical qualities. Were these particular women inspired to run because of the particularly female backlash against the victory of Donald Trump? As their words on the campaign trail demonstrate, the answer is plainly "Yes." The rhetoric of the campaign often called out President Trump directly, and to a greater extent than is usual for an opposing campaign. These six women running for president were in some ways an extension of the #MeToo movement. For example, U.S. senator Amy Klobuchar referenced the Senate's impeachment trial while campaigning in Iowa: "I may be the juror in that chamber, but you are the juror in this election!"[9] U.S. senator Elizabeth Warren, in a CNN Town Hall, was asked by a young woman whether the men in the race "have a better chance of defeating Trump, solely because of their gender?" Warren responded, "I believe they may think so, but they're wrong!" She drew laughter, but as she went on, the mood quickly got serious: "The world changed in 2016 when Donald Trump became president." She pointed to times in history when people who many Americans thought could not be president because they would be breaking down barriers—in 1960, John F. Kennedy, the first Catholic, and in 2008, Barack Obama, the first African American. "This party is better than that,"[10] she said, suggesting that it is time to tear down the barriers of the past that have held women back and elect a woman.

HOW DID THE PRESS COVER SIX WOMEN?

Throughout the primary campaign, the press routinely remarked on the abundance of women, noting it was the first time so many women had run in a presidential primary at once. So many, in fact, that presumably *Vogue* magazine had to make the questionable decision to leave one of the six women out of its cover photo. Excluded was best-selling author Marianne Williamson. Included in the photo were U.S. representative Tulsi Gabbard and U.S. senators Kirsten Gillibrand, Kamala Harris, Amy Klobuchar, and Elizabeth Warren. The excuse offered by the magazine for excluding Williamson: she was not an elected official. In 2016, the Clinton campaign eschewed an appearance in *Vogue*, indicating that a fashion magazine was too frivolous a vehicle for its nominee to pose for. That any of the women at all posed for *Vogue* in 2020 demonstrates that perhaps a cultural shift in attitudes occurred after the 2016 election regarding women candidates for the U.S. presidency and how they can present themselves.

(Then, too, in 2016, the magazine—heretofore synonymous with fashion—had endorsed Clinton for president.) That the women candidates in 2020 willingly agreed to be featured in *Vogue*, and that Williamson complained about being left out, shows that the thinking may have been that all press is good press.

Before 2020, when women ran for president, the press continued to call their bids "the first"—accentuating their novelty and arguably hindering their campaigns. For example, Erica Falk and Kathleen Hall Jamieson contend that "framing their candidates as a 'first' instead of a continuation or extension of a long history of political activism and involvement among women in politics, the press may have promoted the idea that women were less normal and more risky in the political sphere."[11] By February 2020 there were just three women left: Elizabeth Warren, who had a robust summer surge; Amy Klobuchar, who caught on slowly but solidly as the weeks went by, and who placed third in the New Hampshire primary; and Tulsi Gabbard, who was left out of debates and town halls, as her national poll numbers stayed in the low single digits.

Each woman's bid for the presidency contributed something to the study of women and presidential politics. If you believe that good things take time and great things happen all at once, having six women—four senators, a young congresswoman, and a best-selling author—seemed to be an embarrassment of riches. Several factors created an environment that encouraged many—including this robust number of women—to run for the Democratic nomination. Among these were the election of Donald Trump, the #MeToo movement, the high number of women taking office after the 2018 midterm election, and the previous election cycle's nomination of Hillary Clinton. The many candidates in the presidential race prompted the following quip from former U.S. congressman Charlie Dent from Pennsylvania: "At the congressional gym, on any given day I can bump into ten people running for president."[12] The following are those running for the Democratic nomination for president in 2020, ranked by their staying power in the race (in descending order):

- Joe Biden, former vice president and former U.S. senator from Delaware;
- Bernie Sanders, U.S. senator from Vermont;
- Tulsi Gabbard, U.S. representative from Hawaii;
- Elizabeth Warren, U.S. senator from Massachusetts;
- Michael Bloomberg, former New York City mayor;
- Amy Klobuchar, U.S. senator from Minnesota;
- Pete Buttigieg, former mayor of South Bend, Indiana;
- Tom Steyer, hedge fund manager, New York;
- Deval Patrick, former Massachusetts governor;

- Michael Bennett, U.S. senator from Colorado;
- Andrew Yang, founder, Venture for America, New York;
- John Delaney, former U.S. representative from Maryland;
- Cory Booker, U.S. senator from New Jersey and former mayor of former Newark, New Jersey;
- Marianne Williamson, author and founder of Project Angel Food, Los Angeles, California;
- Julian Castro, former secretary of the U.S. Department of Housing and Urban Development, Washington, DC, and former mayor of San Antonio, Texas;
- Kamala Harris, U.S. senator from California;
- Steve Bullock, Montana governor;
- Joe Sestak, former U.S. representative from Pennsylvania;
- Wayne Messam, mayor of Miramar, Florida;
- Beto O'Rourke, former U.S. representative from Texas;
- Tim Ryan, U.S. representative from Ohio;
- Bill De Blasio, New York City mayor;
- Kirsten Gillibrand, U.S. senator from New York;
- Seth Moulton, U.S. representative from Massachusetts;
- Jay Inslee, Washington governor;
- John Hickenlooper, former Colorado governor and former Denver mayor;
- Mike Gravel, former U.S. senator from Alaska;
- Eric Swalwell, U.S. representative from California; and
- Richard Ojeda, former West Virginia state senator.

Indeed, the 2020 Democratic primary race was the largest in American history. Up until 2020, the largest Democratic fields were in 1972 (fifteen candidates) and 1976 (sixteen candidates).[13]

Women candidates for president in 2020 included Tulsi Gabbard, Kirsten Gillibrand, Amy Klobuchar, Kamala Harris, Elizabeth Warren, and Marianne Williamson. Brief biographical sketches of each candidate follow.

U.S. representative Tulsi Gabbard, an Army National Guard veteran who was deployed twice to the Middle East, was first elected to the House in 2012, a decade after she became the youngest person elected to the Hawaii state legislature. She was the first Hindu and the first American Samoan elected to Congress. A composed and articulate speaker, she got into politics in her early twenties and was the youngest female candidate to run in 2020. She distinguished herself rhetorically by taking positions not usually associated with the Democratic Party, let alone the military, such as her noninterventionist views. She boldly asserted that she was the best person to lead the nation, arguing that "we may be sucked into another event more disastrous than the war in the Middle East, and tensions with other nuclear powers are escalating."[14] A public feud with Hillary Clinton during the primary season led to speculation that she was being left out of significant primary media events, such as a television commercial about party unity that featured ten other Democrats, and a CNN Town Hall that was being aired just weeks before the Iowa caucuses and New Hampshire primaries.

Senator Kirsten Gillibrand from New York rose to national prominence when selected to replace Hillary Clinton in the Senate in 2009. Gillibrand, who often paid tribute to her trailblazing grandmother and mother in her speeches, was the most feminist of all the female candidates. As a presidential candidate in 2020, Kirsten Gillibrand emphasized the power of women and became associated most strongly with the #MeToo movement. Her rhetoric underscored her focus on family policies and gender inequities and utilized her own lived experiences as a mother to back up her claims. She often cited the challenges that she faces as a working mother.

Senator Amy Klobuchar of Minnesota came to the attention of many Americans during the hearings held in response to Christine Blasey Ford's accusation of sexual assault against Supreme Court nominee Brett Kavanaugh, when she questioned him about his drinking. A popular three-term senator from Minnesota, Klobuchar often uses rhetoric that includes stories from middle-class people, including her own family, as one of two daughters raised by a school teacher and a newspaper reporter. She often references stories from her own life and the lives of her constituents, including her father's struggle and eventual triumph over alcoholism, the financial challenges and divorce her family faced, and the high cost of education and health care. Acknowledging that her style in debates and speeches is not flashy or especially articulate, Klobuchar underscored that she may not be the "loudest" candidate and stressed that her policies are realistic and doable. She tried to make the case that as a Midwesterner, she represents most Americans.

The presidential bid of Senator Kamala Harris of California was short-lived, especially considering her strong initial launch. An articulate, charismatic campaigner, she was hailed as the "female Obama."[15] But she struggled for months to increase her low poll numbers. A bump in the polls came for her when she called out Joe Biden in a primary debate for his policy against the desegregation of busing in the 1970s. Citing her own experience with busing, her dramatic declaration—"That little girl was me"[16]—became a viral meme. Despite her lackluster presidential showing, she would be back in the limelight as Joe Biden's vice presidential pick.

Senator Elizabeth Warren of Massachusetts rose the highest in the polls and at times challenged Joe Biden for front-runner status. She was often loquacious with her responses to questions, beginning her utterances with a professorial "So . . .," and then flowing into a lengthy explanation of her well-thought-out plans. The crowds for her rallies were large, and she received more press coverage than the other candidates, likely because of her early front-runner status. But her campaign faltered. An especially hard blow came when she failed to win her home state of Massachusetts.

Author Marianne Williamson was often depicted as the outlier candidate, perhaps because she never held political office. But that could have been said of Andrew Yang as well. Articulate and earthy with her responses, her main argument was that only a seismic shift in thinking would right the wrongs of the Trump administration. Most notably, she said that human decency and love are the only qualities that would have a lasting impact on the country at this challenging time.

Although the primary field was initially large, by the beginning of September a number of conventionally qualified candidates began to drop out of the race. Joe Biden was the exception. But those dropping out included Governor Jay Inslee of Washington, Governor John Hickenlooper of Colorado, Governor Steve Bullock of Montana, and Senator Kirsten Gillibrand from New York. (Gillibrand was the first of the six women candidates to leave the race after an eight-month campaign.)

Pivotal primary moments included *The New York Times* endorsement of two women—Amy Klobuchar and Elizabeth Warren—with the *Times* editorial board noting that "the two female senators have released some of the most detailed policy plans of the candidates remaining in the primary campaign, prompting the board to praise each one as the "standard-bearer" for her wing of the party."[17] Another woman, House Speaker Nancy Pelosi, drew the spotlight during the primary race when she played a key role in the impeachment hearing of Donald Trump. Constitutionally the presiding officer of the lower legislative chamber and statutorily second in line to the presidency, after the vice president, Pelosi is the closest figure the United States has had to a woman president. For years she has demonstrated what it means to be a woman in power. When she addressed the Smith College graduation in 2020, remotely because of the Covid-19 pandemic, she extended special greetings from the "House Democratic Caucus, which I'm proud to say is more than sixty percent women, people of color and LGBTQ members."[18]

The impeachment affected three of the 2020 presidential contenders, including two of the women running, who had their primary campaigns sidelined when they had to spend two weeks in January in Washington to serve on the Senate impeachment trial. Senators Bernie Sanders, Elizabeth Warren, and Amy Klobuchar returned to Iowa just a couple of days before the Iowa caucus.

A hearty endorsement of Joe Biden from Congressman Jim Clyburn of South Carolina, right in time for the South Carolina primary, quickly resulted in Pete Buttigieg and Amy Klobuchar dropping out of the race and endorsing

Joe Biden. The race dwindled to only Joe Biden and Bernie Sanders, and finally Sanders withdrew and offered his support to Biden.

Tulsi Gabbard was the last of the women candidates to drop out of the race, citing her need to help the country fight the coronavirus pandemic, and return to her work in the National Guard.

The impeachment of President Trump also held the country spellbound, taking attention away from the primary race. But unlike the coronavirus, the impeachment ended swiftly and left the news cycle. Covid-19 would change the entire campaign: sending Joe Biden to his basement-turned-TV studio and allowing Trump to cast himself as a "wartime" president (his own description, referencing his power as commander in chief to combat the war of Covid-19).

Early during the pandemic, Trump led a task force in a televised presentation to update the American people of the status of the coronavirus, and what the country would do to come to the aid of the millions of people affected by the scourge. Trump had dominated the television news in 2016 with his unorthodox campaign for president; now, Covid-19 gave him another television platform, one that equally gripped the nation. But the virus would prove to be not only deadly for the country but also became a pivotal campaign issue, once Joe Biden became the nominee and charged that President Trump's careless handling of the Covid-19 virus should disqualify him from a second term as president.

This book recounts the bids of six women for president in 2020. Studying the rhetoric of women who have run for president sheds light not only on what happened when they ran but also on the social construction of gender and how it shapes leaders in the United States.

NOTES

1. Patrick Healy and Amy Chozick, "Hillary Clinton Warns of 'Moment of Reckoning' in Speech Accepting Nomination," *The New York Times*, July 28, 2016, https://www.nytimes.com/2016/07/29/us/politics/dnc-hillary-clinton-speech.html ?searchResultPosition=6 (accessed March 6, 2020).

2. Eleanor Clift and Tom Brazaitis, *Madame President: Shattering the Last Glass Ceiling* (New York: Scribner, 2000), 20.

3. David K. Li, "Lock Her Up Chant Breaks Out While Trump Speaks to Veterans Group," *New York Post*, July 26, 2016, https://nypost.com/2016/07/26/lock -her-up-chant-breaks-out-while-trump-speaks-to-veterans-group/ (accessed October 23, 2020).

4. Kelly L. Winfrey and James M. Schnoebelen, "Running as a Woman (or Man): A Review of Research on Political Communicators and Gender Stereotypes." *Review of Communication Research*, 7, January 25, 2019, 109–138, doi: 10.12840/ ISSN.2255- 4165.020.

5. C. L. Bower, "Public discourse and female presidential candidates," in *Anticipating Madam President*, eds. R. P. Watson and A. Gordon (Boulder, CO: Lynne Rienner Publishers, Inc., 2003), 107–116.

6. Linda Will, Karen M. Paget and Glenna Matthews, *Running as a Woman: Gender and Power in American Politics* (New York: The Dree Press, 1994), 106.

7. Richard L. Fox, 2011. "Studying Gender in U.S. Politics: Where Do We Go from Here?," *Politics & Gender* 7(1): 94–99.

8. Ibid.

9. Jane C. Timm, "Iowa caucuses: Klobuchar puts Trump's impeachment trial at center of high-stakes closing pitch," NBC, February 3, 2020. clo https://www.nbcnews.com/politics/2020-election/iowa-caucuses-klobuchar-puts-trump-s-impeachment-trial-center-high-n1128521 (accessed February 6, 2020).

10. "Warren's answer about male candidates' odds draws laughter," CNN Town Hall, February 6, 2020, https://www.cnn.com/videos/politics/2020/02/06/elizabeth-warren-new-hampshire-town-hall-male-candidates-odds-against-trump-sot-vpx.cnn (accessed February 7, 2020).

11. Erica Falk and Kathleen Hall Jamieson, "Changing the Climate of Expectations," in *Anticipating Madam President*, eds. Robert P. Watson and Ann Gordon (Boulder, CO: Lynne Rienner Publishers, 2003), 49.

12. Charlie Dent, conversation, August 1, 2019, Slatington, PA.

13. Ed Kilgore, "Looks Like the 2020 Democratic Presidential Field Could Be the Largest Ever," *New York*, February 13, 2019, https://nymag.com/intelligencer/2019/02/2020-democratic-presidential-field-could-be-the-largest-ever.html (accessed March 23, 2020).

14. Gerry Mullany, "Gabbard Won't Seek Fifth Term in Congress: Possible Third Party Bid for Presidency," *The New York Times*, October 26, 2019, A11.

15. https://www.theweek.in/news/world/2019/01/22/how-kamala-harris-acquiredthe-title-of-female-barack-obama.html (accessed April 30, 2020).

16. Ellie Bufkin, "'That little girl was me': Kamala Harris says she was a victim of Biden's anti-busing racial policies," *The Washington Examiner*, June 27, 2019, https://www.washingtonexaminer.com/news/kamala-harris-says-she-was-a-victim-of-bidens-racial-policies (accessed August 17, 2020).

17. https://www.nytimes.com/2020/01/19/us/politics/amy-klobuchar-elizabeth-warren-new-york-times-endorsement.html (accessed April 30, 2020).

18. Nancy Pelosi, YouTube, 2020 Smith College Commencement Address, May 17, 2020, https://www.youtube.com/watch?v=HJFiJF__RnU (accessed May 18, 2020).

Chapter 1

Tulsi Gabbard

Leading with Aloha[1]

Tulsi Gabbard, born in American Samoa and raised in Hawaii, embodies the spirit of aloha. More than just a greeting, aloha is the spirit of life. Many people understand aloha to mean simply "hello" or "goodbye," but for Gabbard, the term signifies a spirit characterized by compassion, self-sacrifice, and respect. Her deep commitment to personal faith and service stems from her family, her Hindu and Christian upbringing, and her motivation to serve others.

As a soldier in the Hawaii Army National Guard who served in combat zone, Gabbard experienced firsthand the true cost of war. With her experiences informing her views as a presidential candidate, she told voters that she would be personally responsible to the country to not go into war without a clear mission, purpose, and strategy. She recalled a sign that she saw when she was serving in Iraq—"Is Today the Day?"[2]—which reminded her that any day her life could be lost. Serving in the war gave her an anti-war stance, because she felt that too many wars were entered into without a strategic plan, needlessly losing countless lives. She is reminded constantly that she did not lose her life, so she should use it to serve others. When speaking, her voice takes on a novel, righteous tone.

She comes from a big interfaith family and her parents encouraged her and her siblings to be true to themselves and to serve others. They led by example, homeschooling them, being active in the community, and also running for political office. She and her siblings all have Hindu names.

Tulsi Gabbard dropped out of the presidential race in March 2020 and threw her support to former vice president Joe Biden. But she is a young politician who has just begun making a national impact, and she is likely to be back in the spotlight, trying to make a difference because of her commitment to serving others and to enacting the aloha spirit.

When Tulsi Gabbard told CNN political contributor Van Jones that she did, indeed, decide to run for president in 2020, the smiling, self-assured Gabbard put herself on the national political stage. A war veteran of two tours of duty in the Middle East, and a major in the U.S. Army National Guard, Gabbard is an outspoken critic of regime-change wars and the new Cold War. When CBS late-night talk show host Stephen Colbert asked her, "Do you think the Iraq War was worth it?" she pointedly told him, "No." He followed up with "Do you think that our involvement in Syria is worth it?" Again, she directly responded without hesitation, "No."[3]

The youngest of the six women in the presidential primary for 2020, Gabbard began her career as an elected official when she was just twenty-one and elected to the Hawaii state legislature. After two deployments to the Middle East as a soldier in the Hawaii Army National Guard, she returned to serve on the Honolulu City Council. When she ran for president, she was serving her fourth term in Congress.

BRIEF BIOGRAPHY

Gabbard was born on April 12, 1981, in Leloaloa, on American Samoa's main island of Tutila. She is the fourth child in a family of five children, born to Carol and Mike Gabbard, who raised her and her siblings in a multicultural and multi-religion family. Her name is Hindu and means "Holy Basil." Her father is of Samoan and European ancestry and is active in his Catholic church. Her mother, born in Indiana, is a practicing Hindu. Tulsi chose to practice Hinduism as a teenager.[4]

Both her mother and father serve as political inspirations. Her mother, Carol Gabbard, was the first elected official in the family, winning a seat on the Hawaii State Board of Education; her father, Mike Gabbard, ran for and won a seat on the Honolulu City Council before running for and winning a seat in the Hawaii State Senate. He also ran (unsuccessfully) for the U.S. Congress. Her views on some issues, such as same-sex marriage, are different from her parents' views. Her mother notes that Tulsi is her own person whose views are shaped "by her own experiences."[5]

Had Tulsi Gabbard stayed in the 2020 race for U.S. president and won, she would have been the first Hindu president. She is proud to share about her Hindu faith, because she believes that many people have misconceptions about Hinduism. She shares a story of "looking into the eyes of a young girl from Texas who shared with me how she'd always been embarrassed to be Hindu, especially among her non-Hindu friends."[6] In 2016, in a speech at the Reason Rally in Washington, DC, an event held to showcase the presence and power of the nonreligious voting bloc, she said, "Nothing is more important to me, and nothing was more important to our founding fathers, than freedom of religion."[7]

Gabbard is the first native of American Samoa and the first Hindu to be elected to Congress; she took her oath of office with her hand on the Bhagavad Gita, one of Hinduism's most important religious texts. Also, along with Tammy Duckworth, the former U.S. Army lieutenant colonel and current U.S. senator from Illinois, Gabbard is one of the first two female combat veterans in Congress. She is also a lifelong vegetarian, a student of martial arts, and an avid surfer. "Every time I get home for a district work week, I make sure I get out on the water a couple of times for an early-morning session. It recharges the batteries."[8]

In late October 2019, in a video posted on Twitter, Gabbard announced that she would not seek another term in Congress. Her announcement fueled speculation that she would break out of the Democratic pack of presidential candidates and run as an independent. She adamantly denied that she would run as an independent, and in her announcement speech to let her constituents know that she would not seek another term, she offered a message of gratitude, saying, "I'm grateful to all of you—the people of Hawaii—for allowing me the honor of serving you in so many ways over the years. At just twenty-one years old, the people of Ewa Beach and Waipahu entrusted me with their votes, electing me to serve as their state representative at a pivotal time of rapid growth in the community."[9]

She then pivoted to a campaign-style speech, asserting that "Washington, our country, and the world is in dire need of aloha"[10]—a unifying force that motivates her public service—and offering the reasons why she is running for president. "As president, I will immediately begin work to end the new Cold War and nuclear arms race, end our interventionist foreign policy of being the world's police, toppling dictators and governments we don't like, and redirect our precious resources towards serving the needs of the people here at home," she said.[11]

THE RHETORIC OF THE PRESIDENTIAL RACE

When Gabbard launched her presidential race, in February 2019, wearing the traditional Hawaiian lei over her red jacket, she said:

Aloha. Thank you so much.

Growing up here in Hawaii, I loved swimming, surfing, and having fun in this paradise we are lucky to call home.

But I gradually realized that I was actually happiest when I was doing things for other people, doing things to protect our water, oceans, and beaches.

This was a different kind of happiness than what I experienced when just thinking of myself. It was a deeper happiness, that stayed with me.

I knew that no matter what path I chose in life, I wanted service to be the foundation.

I am proud to serve our country as a soldier. I'm a Major in the Army National Guard where I've served for the last fifteen years.[12]

The overarching theme of her presidential speech was service above self. Quoting John F. Kennedy, she said, "Ask not what your country can do for you, ask what you can do for your country."[13]

Gabbard's most significant political communication attribute is that she "doesn't fit neatly into any one established ideology of school of thought."

"I know first-hand the price of war,"[14] she told an interviewer. This overarching theme, the experience of her military career, shapes her entire reason for running for president and her political views.

In an interview on CNN, Tulsi Gabbard articulated her major political stance when she told CNN anchor Jake Tapper that "unless we deal with this cost of war and investing the peace dividend that would come about by making this policy change . . . we will not have the resources that we need to make sure we have health care for all, to make sure that we have the funds to invest in our infrastructure, and to make sure education and housing are affordable."[15]

Further underscoring this view, she later told CNN's Wolf Blitzer that "the United States should not be on a nation-building mission." She went on to explain: "If we're talking about small deployments of Special Forces, troops who are going out there directly to defeat our enemy, defeat ISIS and work with local ground forces to be able to accomplish that mission, then that's something that makes sense. That very different than a large deployment of 10,000 or 100,000 regular ground troops or an occupying force, as we've seen in Iraq."[16]

Her motivation for serving in Congress and running for president is evident in a speech she gave at the University of San Francisco. She said:

We're in a place where we have a government that is not of the people, by the people and for the people, but rather a government that is controlled and influenced by self-serving politicians, greedy corporations and those special interests who can afford to buy their seat at the table as laws are being made.[17]

She often evokes her "aloha" roots in her speeches, explaining that the term is much more than a greeting:

Now a lot of people know Aloha is a word that means hello or goodbye, right? Because this is how we greet each other in Hawaii. But there's a reason why we start our conversations and our gatherings with this word Aloha because there is so much power in what it actually means. When we greet each other with Aloha and we gather in the spirit of Aloha, what we're really saying is I love you, I care for you, I respect you, and I recognize that we are all brothers and sisters, we're all children of God regardless of where we come from or the color of our skin, who we love, how much money we make or don't make, what kind of education we have.[18]

She also evoked the aloha tradition in September 2019, at the Polk County Democrats Steak Fry, long considered an essential Iowa tradition for presidential candidates. She began her speech by saying:

Aloha Iowa Democrats! How you guys doing? You know, in Hawaii when we get these little gentle showers we consider them blessings. Yeah, I feel blessed, I feel grateful to be here to join all of you today at such an important time. Now I start our conversation here with "aloha" because it's important. You know, we're facing increasingly divided times. Self-serving politicians in Washington who are pitting one group of us against the other, pitting one tribe against the other, tearing us apart. And now I start with "aloha" because, not as a way to say hello, but because there's a very powerful meaning here that inspires us in how we can come together.[19]

She went on to say that God is with us all when we say "aloha."

Another example of Gabbard's use of "aloha" occurred when she gave a speech at the Iowa Democratic Wing Ding, an event that raises funds for the Democratic Party in many Iowa counties. As the song "Ain't No Mountain High Enough" played over the sound system, she calmly walked onto the stage and shared how the current Trump administration "breaks her heart," because "we have a president in the White House who is using his position to stoke fear, to stoke racism and to stoke bigotry—all for his own personal gain." Eliciting lively applause, she went on to say, "We are all created equal, and when we focus on this unifying principle, what we in Hawaii call the spirit of aloha, this is what lights the path forward. Aloha means so much more than hello or goodbye."[20]

Drawing on her ethos as a soldier, she called out Democratic rival Kamala Harris early in the primary season, asserting that Harris "is not qualified to serve as commander in chief," adding that "I can say this from a personal perspective as a soldier."[21]

Again she evoked her military service when she asserted that "the president's most important responsibility is serving as commander in chief. I will do so as a soldier who understands the seriousness of this responsibility."[22]

In a speech she gave in late October 2019 in South Carolina, Gabbard argued for criminal justice reform. Lamenting the lack of any kind of significant change to the criminal justice system, she asserted that "one generation after another continues to fall victim to a justice system that is fundamentally unjust. So we think to our pledge of allegiance that we've said over and over throughout our lives, it reminds us that we are '. . . one nation under God, indivisible, with liberty and justice for all.'"[23]

She called out big pharma, for-profit prisons, and criminal justice practices through which "nonviolent drug offenders are arrested, thrown in prison, shackled with a criminal record that will follow them wherever they go forever."[24]

She promised that "as President, I will end this corruption, end private prisons and work to fundamentally transform our prison system."[25]

During the primary debates, Tulsi Gabbard had several notable moments. In the second primary debate, she called out Senator Kamala Harris and questioned her record on criminal justice as attorney general and district attorney. She asserted that Harris "owes an apology to the people" who were impacted by her policies. Gabbard complained that Harris's record as California's attorney general and San Francisco's district attorney included cracking down on truancy, defending the death penalty and several cases of wrongful conviction, and even ignoring survivors of clergy sexual abuse. Gabbard said, "I'm concerned about this record of Senator Harris. She put over 1,500 people in jail for marijuana violations and laughed about it when she was asked if she ever smoked marijuana." She continued, "She blocked evidence that would have freed an innocent man from death row. She kept people in prison beyond their sentences to use them as cheap labor for the state of California, and she fought to keep cash bail system in place that impacts poor people in the worst kind of way."[26]

Gabbard qualified for only five debates, and her poll numbers remained low. She voted "present" on the impeachment vote and explained her choice in a written and recorded statement afterward:

> I am standing in the center and have decided to vote present, because I could not in good conscience vote against impeachment because I believe President Trump is guilty of wrongdoing.

The congresswoman foreshadowed her taped remarks when speaking to an ABC News reporter before the release of the remarks, saying:

"I think impeachment, unfortunately, will only further embolden Donald Trump, increase his support and the likelihood that he'll have a better shot at getting elected, while also seeing the likelihood that the House will lose a lot of seats to Republicans."[27] Gabbard also insisted that her vote was "not a decision of neutrality" and that "thinking about what's politically advantageous, whether for me or for my party, does not enter into my mind around these decisions that have really great consequence."[28]

As the primary season moved toward spring 2020, Gabbard was barely seen on CNN and was being outspent by her rivals on advertising. She appeared several times on Fox News, and in one interview defended President Trump's decision to remove two administration officials from their posts after they testified in the House's impeachment process. She said:

I disagree with so many of Trump's decisions, especially as it relates to foreign policy; I've been very outspoken in that area. . . . Ultimately, whether people like it or not, there are consequences to elections, and the president has, within his purview, to make the decisions about who he'd like serving in his Cabinet.[29]

Criticized for traveling to Syria in 2016 to meet with Bashar Assad, Gabbard defended her choice by saying that it is important to meet with adversaries if "you are serious about pursuing peace."[30]

A RUSSIAN ASSET?

In the fall of 2019, on the podcast *Campaign HQ* hosted by David Plouffe, President Barack Obama's campaign manager in 2008, Hillary Clinton opined that Gabbard was being groomed by Moscow to run as a third-party spoiler candidate in 2020 to help President Trump win reelection.

Plouffe and Clinton discussed hurdles the Democratic nominee would face and compared the 2020 race to Clinton's loss to Trump in 2016. Plouffe asked Clinton about the part third-party candidates, such as Jill Stein of the Green Party, played in 2016, allowing Trump to secure key states. "They are also going to do third-party again," Hillary Clinton asserted. She added, referring to Gabbard, "I'm not making any predictions, but I think they've got their eye on somebody who is currently in the Democratic primary and are grooming her to be the third-party candidate." She further said, "She is a favorite of the

Russians. They have a bunch of sites and bots and other ways of supporting her so far. That's assuming Jill Stein will give it up, which she might not because she is also a Russian asset."[31]

Never one to back down from an assault on her character, Gabbard tweeted back a response to Hillary Clinton: "You, the queen of warmongers, embodiment of corruption, and personification of the rot that has sickened the Democratic Party for so long, have finally come out from behind the curtain," Gabbard wrote, "It's now clear that this primary is between you and me. Don't cowardly hide behind your proxies. Join the race directly."[32] She followed up her Twitter response by filing a defamation lawsuit against Clinton. She asserted in her complaint that Clinton deliberately and maliciously made false statements in an attempt to derail her presidential bid, by alleging that Gabbard is a "Russian asset."[33]

As the primary fight wore on, there was speculation in the press that her feud with Hillary Clinton was costing her valuable press coverage. For example, ten Democratic candidates participated in a television commercial calling for the unity of the party, but Gabbard was not included in the commercial. Ironically, the commercial posits that each of the candidates is running to be the nominee, and no matter who ends up getting it, each person will support the eventual nominee. The commercial states, "Unity is what this moment in history demands of us right now because the stakes have never been higher. As Democrats, we know there is so much more that unites us than divides us. And next year, we have the opportunity to make sure that our shared values are represented."[34] In another apparent snub, CNN did not invite Gabbard to participate in the Town Hall programming that it aired just weeks before the Iowa caucuses. Gabbard commented that she received "no explanation"[35] as to why she was not invited, while candidates polling lower than she were included.

Gabbard is a polished, professional presence and a fierce debater. While she drew attention to herself in the debates for her confident assertions, she still failed to poll well.

GABBARD'S PUBLIC SPEAKING

Tulsi Gabbard has a comportment that is dignified, stoic, and steady. Her words flow in a slightly automated, monotone delivery that sometimes appears detached from what she is saying. But her commitment to public service and to her ideals always comes through. Her military background is evidenced in her erect posture, sustained eye contact, and steady voice. As though waited to be evaluated for her correct delivery she is ultra-poised in her public communication, demonstrating a diligence for precision and polish.

INVENTION

A major theme of Gabbard's speaking is the horror and tragedy of war. She surprised audiences when, as a veteran, she denounced the cost of war, citing her own, lived experiences as a soldier. She said, "I have seen the cost of war firsthand and experienced the consequences of what happens when we have presidents from both political parties in the White House who lack experience and lack that foreign policy understanding, who therefore fall under the influence of the foreign policy establishments and military industrial complex."[36]

In her speeches, she also underscores how native cultures deserve respect. She speaks with urgency about the destruction of war, and despite being the youngest candidate, in combat zones she sharply experienced the feeling that any day could have been her last. This life-shaping experience was one that she recounted often in her speeches, likely because it meant so much to her and shaped her in ways nothing else has. For example, at a dinner event in Los Angeles, she made her way to the stage and spoke briefly, saying:

> My first deployment was at the height of the war in 2005. We were forty miles north of Baghdad. And there was huge sign by one of the main gates that just read: "Is today the day?" It was such a stark reminder that my time could come at any moment. That any day could be my last.[37]

This type of dramatic statement about her war experiences signified that as president she would make the decision to go to war a major focus of her administration. The cost of war in every dimension seemed to be constantly at the top of her mind.

Another theme of many of her speeches is drug decriminalization. While campaigning in New Hampshire in early 2020, she said, "If we take that step to legalize and regulate, then we're no longer treating people who are struggling with substance addiction and abuse as criminals and instead getting them the help that they need."[38] No doubt a major problem in the United States, Gabbard believed that rehabilitation is key to giving people with substance addiction a chance to reform themselves and lead productive lives. She took on big technology companies, too asked for them not to have the oversized influence in society.

DISPOSITION

Tulsi Gabbard frequently organized her ideas by identifying a problem, such as the cost of war, or the marginalization of Native Americans, and offering evidence to support her position. She organizes her speeches clearly and distinctly and is a disciplined speaker, never rambling or interjecting extra information. She stays on point. For example, in a speech she gave in October 29 calling for justice reform, she identified the problem, saying, "We have mass incarceration that has predominantly impacted poor people and communities of color. People's lives ruined because of one mistake . . . while others whose entire careers are built on predatory behavior and the exploitation of the innocent . . . are routinely excused. This is not justice."[39] She then carefully backed up her claim with specific examples, citing cases where rich or privileged people literally got away with crimes while poor and minority people are likely to spend years, if not their entire lives, incarcerated.

STYLE

Tulsi Gabbard's routine use of language in her speeches—her rhetorical style—has several distinct characteristics, including her use of the active voice, direct, even confrontational word choice, personal and inclusive pronouns, and personal, lived experience as evidence of her fitness for leadership. She is unafraid to take on more experienced politicians by citing specific ways that they have not demonstrated leadership, as she did with both Hillary Clinton and Kamala Harris. This evokes a rebellious type of brave communication, not commonly demonstrated in the political correct world of Washington, DC, politics. In this way, Gabbard's style is noticeable and unique.

DELIVERY

A significant and distinct aspect of Tulsi Gabbard's public speaking is her virtually flawless speech delivery. She is notably poised and seemingly unable to be ruffled, often subtly smiling in the beginning of her talk, in a relaxed, composed way, with direct eye contact and a soldier's admirable posture. She favored a white pantsuit, as well as pants with a red suit jacket and jackets in other primary colors. Her dark hair styled straight, she cut an impressive and even regal figure. She is cool and calm as a speaker, sometimes even robotic seeming in her precision. Her tone is often serious and deliberate, not an affable, friendly politician. Her smile drops from her lips when she recounts lessons she learned from deployment, or when she shares other views that are often warnings. She delivers her serious messages in a matter-of-fact and deliberate manner. For example, at a campaign speech in North Dakota, she closed her remarks by saying, "As we stand here tonight, there are thousands of nuclear missiles pointed right at us, and if we were to get an attack, we would have thirty minutes, thirty minutes until we were hit."[40]

MEMORIA

In her deep, relatively emotionless voice, she communicates a resolve for her positions, often from memory and without note cards or a teleprompter. Gabbard has a serious and focused demeanor and almost never trips over words or misspeaks. She is a smooth, deliberate communicator who is in command of her material. Her speeches are carefully constructed and Gabbard delivers them with military precision. She is poised and seemingly unflappable in her presentations.

OBSTACLES TO HER PRESIDENTIAL BID

Tulsi Gabbard struggled to make any significant gains in national political polls. The most media attention of her campaign was a result of Hillary Clinton's assertion that she was a Russian bot. And yet, her youthful, polished, forthright persona suggests that she is just getting started in her political career. Weeks before the New Hampshire primary, she was seen snowboarding, with a relaxed grin, displaying a contemporary, free-spirited athletic image, reminiscent of John Kennedy sailing. Gabbard will likely be on the presidential stage again. Right before she hit the slopes, her responses to reporters suggested that she has a message with appeal and that she is not one to ever give up or walk away from a fight: "People have lost faith, largely, that these institutions, whether in media or in politics, are working for them. And so they're looking for other voices that they can trust and that'll tell them the truth."[41]

AFTER HER PRESIDENTIAL BID

Gabbard did not quickly suspend her campaign, even though it continually struggled to boost her viability. Throughout her campaign, her poll numbers in qualifying national and state polls hovered between zero percent and two percent.[42] And then in mid-March 2020, the coronavirus pandemic provided her with a rhetorical platform from which she could take on a different kind of service. In a video posted to social media on Thursday, March 19, Gabbard said she felt she could better serve the country in the midst of the coronavirus pandemic in her capacity as a major in the Hawaii Army National Guard. Because of this, she announced that she would be suspending her presidential campaign and supporting Joe Biden. "Our nation is facing an unprecedented global crisis that highlights the inextricable bonds of humanity, and how foreign policy and domestic policy are inseparable," she said. "The best way I can be of service at this time is to continue to work for the health and well-being of the people of Hawaii and our country in Congress, and to stand ready to serve in uniform should the Hawaii National Guard be activated."[43]

In 2016, she had resigned her vice-chairmanship at the Democratic National Committee to endorse the presidential campaign of Senator Bernie Sanders. But in 2020 she endorsed Joe Biden, citing her relationship with his late son Beau, who had served in the Delaware Army National Guard. "Although I may not agree with the vice president on every issue, I know that he has a good heart and is motivated by his love for our country and the American people," she said. "I'm confident that he will lead our country guided by the spirit of aloha—respect and compassion—and thus help heal the divisiveness that has been tearing our country apart."[44]

After the first Democratic debate, Gabbard was briefly the most searched-for candidate on Google.[45] She made an impact on voters and was especially exciting for young voters looking for someone who represents bipartisan passion. Tulsi Gabbard is a young politician whose future is wide open. By running for president in 2020 she changed the rhetoric of presidential politics by representing military women, the spirit of aloha, and in so doing she attracted national attention, giving herself name recognition that could prove invaluable in the future. She also gave all the skills necessary for political success a trial run; she has proven to be an independent thinker, an articulate speaker, and a youthful voice with military experience and a worldview that may prove attractive to voters in years to come.

NOTES

1. Forgey, Quint, "Tulsi Gabbard Says She Won't Run for Re-Election," Politico, October 25, 2019, https://www.politico.com/news/2019/10/25/tulsi-gabbard-wont -run-congress-reelection-2020-057222 (accessed October 26, 2019).

2. Ibid.

3. Stephen Colbert Show, interview with Tulsi Gabbard, Mar 12, 2019, https:// www.youtube.com/watch?v=i0jnKb8MDks (accessed July 16, 2019).

4. "Raising Hawaii's Next Political Star," Hawaii News Television Show, Now .https://www.hawaiinewsnow.com/story/20929142/the-gabbards-raising-hawaiis -next-political-star-5pm/ (accessed July 16, 2019).

5. Ibid.

6. Gabbard, Tulsi, commentary for Religion News Service, January 26, 2019.

7. Gabbard, Tulsi, speech at Reason Rally, Washington, DC, June 2016.

8. Powers, John. "Tulsi Gabbard Is Making a Splash," *Vogue*, June 24, 2013 https://www.vogue.com/article/making-a-splash-is-tulsi-gabbard-the-next-demo- cratic-party-star (accessed October 21, 2019).

9. Petersen, Beatrice, and Meg Cunningham, "Hawaii Rep. Tulsi Gabbard says she won't run for re-election in her district; Gabbard announced Thursday night she would focus solely on her presidential bid." ABC News, October, 25, 2019, https://abcnews.go.com/Politics/hawaii-rep-tulsi-gabbard-run-election-district/story?id=66526443 (accessed January 20, 2020).

10. Ibid.

11. Ibid.

12. Gabbard, Tulsi, presidential announcement speech, February 2, 2019, https://www.tulsi2020.com/press/2019-02-02-tulsi-gabbards-full-speech-presidential-campaign-launch (accessed January 27, 2020).

13. Ibid.

14. Iverson, Kim, interview with Tulsi Gabbard, April 6, 2019, https://www.youtube.com/watch?v=5ybH9p2uFiE (accessed July 16, 2019).

15. Tulsi Gabbard, interview with Jake Tapper, CNN "The Lead with Jake Tapper," April 11, 2019, from "Why I Fight" Tulsi Gabbard, Kindle book, 2019, Resistance Publishing.

16. Gabbard, Tulsi, The Situation Room with Wolf Blitzer, December 1, 2015.

17. Gabbard, Tulsi, speech at University of San Francisco, March 16, 2019.

18. Ibid.

19. Gabbard, Tulsi, speech, Iowa Democratic Steak Fry, September 21, 2019, https://awpc.cattcenter.iastate.edu/2019/09/27/iowa-democratic-steak-fry-sept-21-2019-4/ (accessed January 22, 2020).

20. Gabbard, Tulsi, speech at Iowa Wing Ding, https://www.youtube.com/watch?v=Vf0mEOAceLs (accessed January 24, 2020).

21. Rozsa, Matthew, "Tulsi Gabbard says Harris is 'Not Qualified to Serve,'" Salon, July 24, 2019.

22. Gabbard, Tulsi, presidential announcement speech, February 2, 2019, https://www.c-span.org/video/?c4777775/representative-tulsi-gabbard-presidential-campaign-announcement (accessed July 16, 2019).

23. Gabbard, Tulsi, speech, Justice for All, Oct. 29, 2019, October 29, 2019, South Carolina, TulsiGabbard.com (accessed March 19, 2020).

24. Ibid.

25. Ibid.

26. Saul, Stephanie, "Tulsi Gabbard Says Kamala Harris Should Apologize for Record as Prosecutor," *The New York Times*, July 31, 2019, https://www.nytimes.com/2019/07/31/us/politics/kamala-harris-prisoners-tulsi-gabbard.html (accessed October 29, 2019).

27. Rozsa, Matthew, Tulsi Gabbard: Impeachment "increased the likelihood that Donald Trump will remain the president," Salon, December 31, 2019. https://www.salon.com/2019/12/31/tulsi-gabbard-impeachment-increased-the-likelihood-that-donald-trump-will-remain-the-president/ (access January 16, 2020).

28. Ibid.

29. Neal, Spencer, "There Are Consequences to Elections," February 10, 2020, Washington Examiner, https://www.washingtonexaminer.com/news/there-are-consequences-to-elections-tulsi-gabbard-defends-trump-firing-of-vindman (accessed February 15, 2020).

30. Gabbard, Tulsi, interview with Kasie Hunt of NBC, February 6, 2019.

31. Pearce, Tim, "Hillary Clinton Says Tulsi Gabbard is a Russian Asset," The Washington Examiner, October 18, 2019, https://www.washingtonexaminer.com/news/hillary-clinton-says-tulsi-gabbard-is-a-russian-asset-groomed-to-ensure-trump-re-election (accessed October 18, 2019).

32. Beggin, Riley, "Tulsi Gabbard calls Hillary Clinton 'the queen of warmongers' in her latest clash with top Democrats," Vox, October 19, 2019, https://www.vox.com/policy-and-politics/2019/10/19/20922122/hillary-clinton-tulsi-gabbard-queen-war-mongers-russia-2020-election (accessed October 21, 2019).

33. Gabbard, Tulsi, 2020 Website, https://www.tulsi2020.com/press/2020-01-22-rep-tulsi-gabbard-files-lawsuit-against-hillary-clinton-over-defamatory-statements (accessed January 24, 2020).

34. "Ten Presidential Candidates Featured; Gabbard Not Invited," The Daily Wire, December 24, 2019. https://www.dailywire.com/news/dnc-promotes-unity-in-new-ad-with-10-presidential-candidates-gabbards-not-invited (accessed January 30, 2020).

35. Concha, Joe, "Gabbard Says She Received No Reason," The Hill, January 29, 2020. https://thehill.com/homenews/campaign/480441-gabbard-says-shes-received-no-reason-from-cnn-for-non-invitation-to-town (accessed January 30, 2020).

36. Rozsa, Matthew, "Tulsi Gabbard says Democratic rival Kamala Harris 'is not qualified to serve as commander-in-chief,'" Salon, July 24, 2019. https://www.salon.com/2019/07/24/tulsi-gabbard-says-democratic-rival-kamala-harris-is-not-qualified-to-serve-as-commander-in-chief/ (accessed March 25, 2020).

37. Bowles, Nellie, "Gabbard, a Soldier Who Is Serious About Peace," *The New York Times*, August 3, 2019, A-1.

38. Angell, Tom, "Tulsi Gabbard Endorses Legalizing Drugs," Forbes.com, January 19, 2020. https://www.forbes.com/sites/tomangell/2020/01/19/tulsi-gabbard-endorses-legalizing-drugs/#776ea3396ed4 (accessed March 25, 2020).

39. Tulsi Gabbard, Justice for All—Oct. 29, 2019, October 29, 2019—South Carolina https://awpc.cattcenter.iastate.edu/2019/11/04/justice-for-all-oct-29-2019/ (accessed August 13, 2020).

40. Bowels, Nellie, "Gabbard, A Soldier Who Is Serious About Peace," *The New York Times*, August 3, 2019, A-1.

41. Jones, Lloyd, "Tulsi Gabbard Parries Sun's Questions And Then Heads for the Slopes," The Sun, January 28, 2020, https://www.conwaydailysun.com/news/local/gabbard-parries-sun-s-questions-then-hits-the-slopes/article_cef72df0-4206-11ea-93e6-db5d211fe641.html (accessed January 30, 2020).

42. Russonello, Giovanni, "Scramble for Name Recognition Deep Inside the Margin of Error," *The New York Times*, October 5, 2019, A10.

43. Lerer, Lisa, and Maggie Astor, "Gabbard Drops Out of Presidential Race," *The New York Times*, March 19, 2020. https://www.nytimes.com/2020/03/19/us/politics/tulsi-gabbard-drops-out.html?action=click&module=Latest&pgtype=Homepage (accessed March 20, 2020).

44. Ibid.

45. Wakabayashi, Daisuke, "Gabbard Sues Google, Saying It Stifled Her Speech," *The New York Times*, July 16, 2019, B3.

Chapter 2

Kirsten Gillibrand

*The "#MeToo Senator," An Advocate
for Women's Rights from a Family
of Trailblazing Women*

Kirsten Gillibrand seemed destined for a nontraditional path all her life. She had strong female role models in both her maternal grandmother and her mother, and her own perfectionist nature set her on a path of private school and vast international travel before she was even out of high school. Her idea of what professional life might look like for her was broadened by an Ivy League college education and after that, law school. But it didn't take long for her life as a partner in a blue-chip law firm to give her the gnawing feeling that something was amiss. She found inspiration in First Lady Hillary Clinton, who was also forging a nontraditional path and encouraging other women to take a seat at the table in the halls of power with her to make lasting changes. The types of changes that resonated most with Gillibrand were those that impacted her and thousands of other working women: equal pay, calling out sexism and misogyny, and worse, sexual assault. Fighting for affordable childcare and better schools and health care became her main issues, no doubt born from her own, lived experiences and those of her female friends who, like her, were hoping to break out of the personal and professional limitations that many of their female ancestors had to face.

U.S. senator Kirsten Gillibrand's presidential announcement in New York City was a masterful combination of images and sounds. Gillibrand took the stage, her blonde bob blowing in the wind, to the sounds of Lizzo's "Good as Hell," an ode to independent, self-confident women: "Come now, come dry your eyes. You know you a star, you can touch the sky. I know that it's hard, but you have to try."[1] Gillibrand hugged her longtime friend and college roommate, actress Connie Britton, who had just given Gillibrand a warm introduction, and took her place at the lectern. A giant American flag was the backdrop, and the Trump International Hotel & Tower—a testament to "greed and corruption," Gillibrand said—loomed nearby. "The people of this country deserve a president who is worthy of your bravery, a president who not only sets an example, but follows yours," Gillibrand continued. "Your bravery inspires me every day, and that is why I'm running for president of the United States."[2]

A LIFE OF POSSIBILITIES AND AMBITIONS
SHAPED BY STRONG FEMALE ROLE MODELS

Long before Kirsten Gillibrand ran for president, she would often speak about the strong women in her family: her lawyer mother, with a black belt in karate, and her New York political kingmaker grandmother, both known as "Polly." Her mother, who was one of only three women in her law school graduating class, took her criminal law exam two days after she gave birth to Kirsten's older brother Douglas. A year and a half later, she stood for the New York state "character and fitness evaluation," part of the New York bar exam, three days before Kirsten was born. Her maternal grandmother, Polly Noonan, was a legend in New York politics; nobody became anyone in Albany politics without gaining her good graces. A founder of the Albany Democratic Women's Club, she "never backed down from an argument."[3] In 2018, she was immortalized in an off-Broadway play called *The True*.[4] To say that Gillibrand had strong female role models her whole life is an understatement, because in addition to her mother and her grandmother, she moved within a circle of influential families through her private schooling, and would regularly refer to classmates who inspired her, as her political star ascended.

On the campaign trail, and in her best-selling 2015 book, *Off the Sidelines*—a feminist "call to action" and memoir—Gillibrand recounted inspiring stories of strong women and urged women to confront sexist pitfalls and boldly step into the political arena. In her book, she credits none other than political trailblazer Hillary Clinton with changing her life's course from corporate law to politics. "The voice that motivated me to take my life in a new direction came from a woman in a pink suit." On September 5, 1995, Hillary Clinton, then still First Lady, spoke at the fourth World Conference on Women in Beijing, China."[5] At the time, Gillibrand felt that her job in corporate law in Manhattan was not her true calling. Because she had spent some of her college years in China, as an Asian studies major, Gillibrand felt that Clinton's speech put her "back in touch"[6] with her childhood dream of being in politics. It was a pivotal moment for Gillibrand, who then began exploring what a political future for herself might look like. It was as though the confluence of her strong, woman-centered upbringing converged with both her ennui with her law firm career and the trailblazing, inspirational rhetoric of an Ivy League–educated First Lady who would not be bound to the traditional constraints of a politician's wife.

Quintessential Suburban Family Life

Kirsten Elizabeth Rutnik was born on December 9, 1966, in Albany, New York, the daughter of Polly Edwina (Noonan) and Douglas Paul Rutnik. Both her parents are attorneys, and her father has also worked as a lobbyist. She has an older brother, Douglas Rutnik, and a younger sister, Erin Rutnik Tschantret. By all accounts, her childhood was comfortable, even idyllic— her mother providing for her a role model of what a working wonder woman could be: fully engaged in her professional career, while still enjoying hobbies and being an attentive and caring mother figure, managing household duties that included baking and shuttling children to after school activities. It seems as though her mother's "do-it-all" approach anticipated the superwoman trend of the 1980s' second-wave feminism, when many women strove to be everything to everyone.

Senator Gillibrand graduated in 1984 from the Emma Willard Academy in Troy, New York—the first all-women's high school in the United States. She was given the push to choose the boarding school over the public high school when a family friend sat her down and pointed out that attending an all-women's school would give her "excellence and the exposure to young women from across the globe."[7] It proved to be a life-changing advice, as Gillibrand noted that through her high school friends she met girls from "South America, Saudi Arabia, and South Korea. She also had the privilege of traveling extensively while in high school, taking school-related trips to France, Spain, north Africa and Russia on school exchange programs each spring."[8] This first-class high school education resonated well with the demands for achievement she placed upon herself, self-identifying as a person who was hoping always for "a gold star," and her father nicknamed her "Loudmouth," shortening it to just "Mouth," recognizing that she was "too much, too loud."[9] But her mother saw in young Kirsten qualities that she shared with both her mother and grandmother: sheer will and determination. Gillibrand acknowledged that because of the support she received from her mother, she felt the freedom to set her own course.

Benefiting from the strong female role models in her family as well as the world-class education she received at Emma Willard Academy, Gillibrand thrived at college and was well prepared for law school. A magna cum laude graduate of Dartmouth College in 1988, she went on to receive her law degree from the UCLA School of Law in 1991 and served as a law clerk on the Second Circuit Court of Appeals. By her own accounts she was a determined, overachieving student and a strong advocate for herself. She had the support of family and friends, and advice, even about how to "brand" herself, years before personal branding became a widely popularized concept. In her youth and throughout college, Kirsten was known by the nickname "Tina," but a judge in Albany advised her that going by Kirsten, not Tina, would serve her better. Later she consulted another judge who gave her the same advice, and so she readopted her given name and used it exclusively—dropping the nickname that might be perceived as cute but childish, more suited to a little girl. By the time she became nationally known, Kirsten was the name that was attached to her—signifying her maturity and professionalism. She reflected, "I realized that, for better or for worse, something as simple as whether you went by a nickname could impact how seriously you were taken."[10]

One can easily imagine the strong impression Hillary Clinton made on Gillibrand during her young professional life, when she saw the former First Lady (and later the first female presidential nominee) speak about women's rights at the 1995 conference on women in Beijing. "Women's rights are human rights," Clinton asserted, "and human rights are women's rights." Clinton's words intensified the passion for women's rights that Gillibrand had been raised with, and the fierce independence she felt in high school, college, and law school. At that point in her career, her work at the law firm was starting to lose its luster. As Gillibrand searched for a new life path, Clinton's words stirred in her the fire of her youth, when she imagined for herself a life of political action as a political player—a candidate—like the candidates her grandmother Polly helped to get elected. Why couldn't she be a political candidate? While her grandmother was helping people to get elected, there were very few women in politics. But Kirsten grew up at a time when roles for women were changing, and she had every right to think that she could run and be elected. This was the time in her life when she began to shift her mind from corporate law to politics.

After working as an attorney in Manhattan for more than a decade, Gillibrand was offered a job as special counsel to the U.S. secretary of Housing and Urban Development by Andrew Cuomo, during the Clinton administration. Cuomo wanted her enough to say, "I'll pay you the highest salary I can under the federal rules, because I know you're leaving a well-paying job."[11] Gillibrand accepted the position, which started her on her career in politics.

At about this time, having also become a political donor and joined The Women's Leadership Forum, an organization that supports Democratic nominees for president, Gillibrand heard Hillary Clinton say, "Decisions are being made every day in Washington, and if you are not part of those decisions, you might not like what they decide and you'll have no one to blame but yourself."[12] This action-oriented challenge from Clinton spurred Gillibrand to think that electoral politics was going to be her ambition. It was at this time that she got married and began to play a more active role in Democratic politics. She began to put herself into Hillary Clinton's circle, feeling that she could reach out to Clinton to ask for advice and guidance when needed.

At Clinton's request, she held a political fundraiser for young women in her professional orbit and worked on the Clinton's 2000 Senate campaign. Gillibrand began to feel not only inspired to promote the politics of Hillary Clinton but also connected enough to feel as though she could be a political candidate herself. She was eyeing opportunities to run for political office, and in 2006 she took on a four-term GOP incumbent and won. That's when the former blue-chip law firm partner's career as a politician truly began in earnest. She was elected to Congress to represent New York's twentieth congressional district, a conservative district in upstate New York. She was reelected in 2008 and began to make a national name for herself. She proved a skillful and successful fundraiser, raising $7.3 million during her two House of Representative campaigns, overcoming an obstacle that often stops women running for political office—the difficulty of bringing in enough money to fuel a campaign. Ellen Malcolm, the founder of the women's Democratic fundraising group EMILY's List, says admiringly about Gillibrand: "Nobody ever would have taken her race seriously if it hadn't been for her tenacious work raising money."[13] She earned a reputation in Congress for being smart, thorough, and ambitious. She earned the nickname "Tracy Flick" after the perfectionist, blonde, and blue-eyed fictional character in the 1999 film *Election*. Played by Reese Witherspoon, the plucky, determined Flick would stop at nothing to achieve her goals.

After the 2008 presidential election, Barack Obama chose Hillary Clinton as his secretary of state, leaving an opening for Clinton's influential U.S. Senate seat. It seemed an opportune moment for Gillibrand, and though several others were considered for the post, New York governor David Paterson chose Gillibrand to fill the high-profile Senate seat, casting her into the national spotlight. Testing her political talent and staying power, Gillibrand won a special election in 2010 to keep the seat. Further proving her political acumen, she was reelected in 2012 and 2018. Her national political star was on the rise, and she appeared often on national television news outlets, representing the Democratic Party and sharing her views about key legislative issues.

Kirsten Gillibrand frequently championed legislation for women, and, using feminist political rhetoric, she often drew from her own, lived experiences. She spearheaded issues such as paid medical leave, women's reproductive health, and the rights of sexual assault survivors.[14] She was also the first of the 2020 candidates to release her tax returns to the public. She was better known than most of the senators running for president, likely due to the high profile of New York as well as the prominence of a Senate seat formerly held by Hillary Clinton.

In her speeches and in her memoir, Gillibrand shares her own struggles of juggling her expanding political life with her growing family, as she welcomed two sons who needed her attention—once, even, when a call to the Senate floor for an early-evening vote required her to leave them for a few minutes in a colleague's office. The solution was that she would stand at the far Senate door and lean in her head to vote while still holding her sons' hands—or, as she put it, "what every working mother wants."[15] Her challenges to raise her children while still fulfilling her professional duties reminded her of both the progress that women have made, and the significant challenges women still face to enjoy both a full home life and professional life. Her rhetoric and legislative efforts often focus on this particular tension.

Rhetoric of the Presidential Race 2020

The groundswell of interest in more women running for office can be traced to the day after the presidential inauguration of Donald J. Trump, when more and more women were marching, speaking out, and being encouraged to run for political office. There was a lot of backlash against Trump, especially from women, because he publicly bragged about assaulting women, and because many women came forward to accuse him of sexual misconduct. It was appalling to many women, especially those who have fought publicly for the rights of women and girls, to see Donald Trump win the presidency over Hillary Clinton. Kirsten Gillibrand told a reporter that she "woke up and bawled" the day after the 2016 election when she realized that Donald Trump was the new president. Instead of celebrating the election of the first woman president of the United States, as she had hoped to do, she found herself distraught and thinking of ways to rise up and make her voice heard. So it was hardly surprising, then, when Kirsten Gillibrand, a feminist overachiever with a history of successful political engagement, announced the formation of an exploratory committee for the 2020 presidential race in January 2019 on *The Late Show with Stephen Colbert*. She said, excitedly, "I'm filing an exploratory bid for the president of the United States—tonight!" Consistent with her Senate campaign, she underscored the need for more support for families, health care, and education when citing her main reason to run for president: "As a young mom I'm gonna to fight for other people's kids as hard as I'll fight for my own, which is why I believe that health care is a right, not a privilege. Better public schools for our kids, because it shouldn't matter what block you are born on."[16] Her answers were measured and sounded rehearsed and polished; at the same time, her telegenic appearance clearly highlighted her exuberance in making her announcement.

Gillibrand did not ask voters to vote for her simply because she is a woman, but the main campaign message she put forth during her brief presidential bid was the most feminist of all the candidates running (men and women). Repeatedly, she used her own, lived experiences as a "young mom" during her campaign. The use of feminist tropes can be problematic for women political candidates, because so often, voters hear only brief "sound bites" of a candidate's overall vision. She gave the first formal speech of her campaign to hundreds of supporters in March 2019, outside the Trump International Hotel & Tower in midtown Manhattan.

Calling the Trump building a "shrine to greed, division, and vanity," Gillibrand asked her supporters to look at it as a sign of greed. "Our president is a coward."[17] With the wind blowing and a red, white, and blue U.S. flag as a backdrop, Gillibrand argued, "Trump wants you to believe he is strong, but he is not!"[18] She went on to forcefully declare, "We deserve a president who is brave," building upon her slogan "Brave Wins," which implied that it is brave for women—or at least for her—to run for president, and that America must "listen to what Lincoln called the better angels of our nature."[19]

Her slogan, "Brave Wins," is also derived from a children's book she cowrote, *Bold & Brave: Ten Heroes Who Won Women the Right to Vote*, about trailblazing suffragist women. She concluded her speech by saying that "Americans prove that brave wins from their bravery every single day."[20] Citing them as exemplars of bravery, Gillibrand gave a shout-out to the victims and survivors of the shooting at Marjory Stoneman Douglas High School in Parkland, Florida; the children of undocumented immigrants known as the Dreamers; sexual assault survivors who raise their voices; the millions of Americans speaking out against the current administration's policies; and the "formerly 'well-behaved' women" who ran for office. This last was a reference to the unprecedented number of women who were elected to Congress in the 2018 midterms. She concluded her announcement speech by saying that all the brave people in America have given her the bravery to run for president.

It was an inspired location and a strong introduction into the presidential race for Kirsten Gillibrand, certainly one of the better-known women in the race. Because of the location of the speech, the inspirational language she used, and her promise to overturn the Trump agenda, her overarching theme of speaking up and speaking out against President Trump, and her effort to galvanize everyone who is at the opposite end of the political spectrum from him, were good rhetorical moves.

At an MSNBC town hall forum in Michigan, Gillibrand shared with host Chris Hayes her view for America. Confidently, she asserted, "I believe I'm the best candidate to take on President Trump, because I have the vision of what actually needs to be done in this country."[21] She continued, with a rapid-fire delivery, barely taking a breath ticking down all the things Americans want, in her view, such as health care; improved education and affordable, high-quality college; and solid employment. When Chris Hayes tried to interrupt her to ask about her record, she interrupted him, complaining that she did not get to finish. She recounted her successes in Congress, and her ability to win elections, even citing percentage points. She underscored her successes in getting bills passed, and finally, the host, Chris Hayes, was able to ask her about her changing record, raising a criticism that had been repeatedly made against her: that is, that she won a relatively conservative district with more conservative positions, especially on gun control, than she was now espousing as a presidential candidate. Ever the assertive debater, Gillibrand put her more consistent and liberal policies out front by reminding Hayes and the audience that she also ran on Medicare for All, and getting out of Iraq, but that she "should have done more."[22] This idea that she could have done more is a point of contention for many seasoned politicians who are called on their previous policies; it may also have framed her, in the minds of many listening, as just another politician with more bluster than true motivational rhetoric.

She resorted to her familiar feminist rhetoric when she told Hayes, "And you know, my mother didn't just cook the Thanksgiving turkey, she shot the Thanksgiving turkey. So I came from a different lens. But what—what I regret is that I should have cared more about ending gun violence in other places."[23] She addressed audience questions about keeping jobs in the United States, childcare, making college more affordable, the student debt crisis, the opioid crisis, immigration, and healthy air and water, and asserted that "the American people want national paid leave. Let's start there. We even have a president who I agree with on basically nothing talking about the need for paid leave."[24]

As the town hall came to a close, Hayes raised another issue that had been getting a lot of attention: her call for Al Franken, fellow Democratic senator, to resign after allegations of sexual harassment came out against him. And then in light of a *New York Times* story about a staffer on her own staff who complained about sexual harassment from someone else on her staff and fought—and quit in protest of the handling of that issue which she felt was not handled well. Gillibrand responded that she believes society must value women. She went on to say, "It is so important that we value women, which is why when a woman or a man comes forward who has an allegation of sexual assault or sexual harassment that you believe them, and that you do a full, thorough investigation so that justice is possible."[25]

Gillibrand continued:

I've been taking on this cause throughout my Senate career, whether it happens in the U.S. military, where so many survivors are disbelieved and not just disbelieved but they're retaliated against. I take it on, on college campuses, because there are colleges across America who'd rather shove it under the rug than have transparency and accountability. I take it on in Congress, passing—with the help of many colleagues, including [U.S. senator] Ted Cruz—a new sexual harassment bill for how Congress deals with sexual harassment. In terms of my own office, the woman who came forward, she was believed, her allegations were taken seriously, they were fully investigated thoroughly and immediately. Her allegations did not rise to sexual harassment, but we did find evidence of derogatory comments. The person that she alleges against was punished and this employee was dearly valued. I told her that she was loved by us, by our office, by me personally, I hugged her, and she was deeply valued. In terms of Senator Franken, it was a very hard issue for so many Democrats, because the truth is, we miss him and people loved him. But he had eight credible allegations against him of sexual harassment for groping, two of them since he was a Senator and the eighth one that came out was a congressional staffer. And I had a choice to make whether to stay silent or not, whether to say it's not OK with me, and I decided to say that. Now, Senator Franken was entitled to whatever type of review or process he wanted, he could have stuck it out, stayed in the Senate, gone through his ethics committee investigation for as long as he wants, forget how many months. He could have sued all of the eight women who came out against him. Those were his choices. But I had to make my choice. Now, I am a mother of boys and the conversations I was having at home at the time were very upsetting. Because Theo [Gillibrand's son] said to me, "Mom, why are you so tough on Al Franken?" And as a mother I had to be really clear, it is not OK for anyone to grope a woman anywhere on her body without her consent, it is not OK to forcibly kiss a woman ever without her consent. It was not OK for Senator Franken, and it is not OK for you, Theo, ever. So I needed to have clarity. And if there are a few Democratic powerful donors who are angry, because I stood up for women who came forward with allegations of sexual harassment, that's on them.[26]

In another campaign town hall speaking event, in late May 2019, Gillibrand appeared on the Fox network with host Chris Wallace. It was surprising to see Gillibrand on Fox, since the network is seen as a platform for conservative politics; however, it became clear, as Gillibrand began speaking, that she had an agenda of her own. She used the opportunity to appear on the conservative network to accuse Fox of setting up a false narrative in the abortion debate. Wallace, seemingly upset with her grandstanding on one particular issue and complaining about Fox's coverage, chided Gillibrand on the spot, saying that her attack against the network was not polite, noting that the network had invited her on the show to share her views for her presidential bid, not to create an opportunity to shame the network for its coverage on abortion. Wallace said, "I understand that maybe to make your credentials with the Democrats who are not appearing on Fox News, you are going to attack us. I'm not sure it's frankly very polite when we've invited you to be here."[27] Gillibrand continued undaunted by Wallace's comment and said, "OK, I'll do it in polite way. I will do it in a polite way. But—the debate about whether or not women should have reproductive freedom has turned into a red-herring debate. And what happens on Fox News is relevant because they talked about infanticide for 6.5 hours," she said. "Six point five hours, right before President Trump's State of the Union mentioned it thirty-five times." Infanticide "doesn't happen, it's illegal, it's not a fact," she said. "That is not the debate of what access to reproductive care in this country."[28]

A week after she appeared on Fox with Chris Wallace, Gillibrand followed up by giving a speech at the Iowa Hall of Fame event where she reminded her audience of Wallace's reprimand that she was "not very polite" to bring up Fox's coverage of abortion during the town hall. She began her speech: "Not. Very. Polite. That's what I was told I was by a Fox News host at the town hall I did in Iowa last week, because I spoke out about the nationwide assault on women's reproductive freedom. Not very polite? You got that one right! Because if Fox News takes issue with me demanding the fundamental, human rights for women, 50 percent of America—I must be doing something right!"[29] Referring to herself again as a "formerly well-behaved woman," she continued, "Luckily, I'm not alone. I proudly count myself among the formerly well-behaved women fighting back. The women in this room, the men who love us. We are rising up and we are demanding our rights and our voices. Women are on fire in America today."[30]

She went on to shout, very much a rallying cry: "We have marched! We have organized! We have run for office and we have won. Because of women, we flipped the U.S. House of Representatives and sent more than one hundred women to Congress!"[31]

She swung back to the theme of her speech, continuing her response to being called not very polite and landing on her "Brave Wins" slogan:

Now is not the time to be polite! Now is not the time for small steps! Now it's time to fight like hell! To the pundits who STILL say: "Can a woman really win?" YES! Of course, we can. President Trump's kryptonite is a strong woman who stands up for what she believes in. We know women leaders across the globe actually have faster-growing economies . . . are more inclusive, tolerant and collaborative. When women lead, we get things done. But with a woman at the head of the table. Now is not the time to settle for the status quo or to compromise or to be polite. Now is the time to be brave! Because when hope rises, fear loses . . . and "Brave Wins"! God Bless Iowa![32]

Gillibrand's fiery, lawyerly rhetoric was also evident on the debate stage, where a crowded primary field of candidates jockeyed for the national press attention a debate brings. At the first primary debate, when asked what she would do first as president, she drew attention to herself and elicited laughter when she said, "The first thing I will do as president of the United States will be to Clorox the Oval Office." The second thing she would do would be to "re-engage on global climate change."[33]

While debating, Gillibrand brought up a short newspaper opinion piece published in 1981. Former vice president Joseph R. Biden Jr., at the time a U.S. senator representing Delaware, made the case that using incentives such as tax credits to encourage high-earning parents to send their kids to day care would lead to "the deterioration of the family," among other things. Dramatically, Gillibrand looked over at Biden and said, pointing her finger:

> I want to address the vice president directly. When the Senate was debating middle-class affordability for childcare, he wrote an op-ed. He voted against it, the only vote. But, when he—he wrote an op-ed, was that he believed that women working outside the home would create the "deterioration" of family. He also said that women who were working outside the home were avoiding "responsibility."[34]

Gillibrand asserted that Biden's op-ed was evidence of his opposition to working mothers, although previously Gillibrand praised Biden for his advocacy of women's issues. This is an example of Gillibrand seeming opportunistic with her rhetoric, but her record points in another direction. As the exchange lumbered on, Biden defended his record on gender equality and accused Gillibrand of hitting his record on women just because she was running for president. "I'm passionate about the concern, making sure women are treated equally," he said. "I don't know what's happened except you're now running for president."

Gillibrand repeatedly went back to the "deterioration of the family" quote.

As the moderators tried to cut her off, Gillibrand told Biden, "You said women working outside the home would lead to the deterioration of family. . . . Either he no longer believes it . . ."

Biden finally offered, "I never believed it."[35]

Overall, however, Gillibrand's debate performances were not memorable, especially in such a crowded field. Her efforts to grab the spotlight could be described as opportunistic and a bit desperate, especially since they largely fell flat.

Media Frames

Gillibrand was dubbed the "#MeToo senator" because of her association with the movement that swept the nation after the election of Donald Trump and continued as many powerful men in politics, entertainment, sports, and business were accused of sexual harassment or assault. Gillibrand's advocacy for survivors of sexual harassment and violence became a major media narrative that framed her presidential bid—one she did not back down from. It could be argued that she embraced it, since she was and continues to be unapologetic about her position on Al Franken and Bill Clinton. She usually cites her maternal responsibility to her sons to let them know that it is unacceptable to treat women the way that Franken and Clinton did. Her position was unpopular, though arguably the right one. However, perhaps because Franken and Clinton are two popular men, Gillibrand seemed to get no credit for her unyielding stance, however noble and just. The press often mentioned her support for ousting Franken and her comment that Bill Clinton should have resigned in the wake of the Monica Lewinsky scandal. Those issues became central to her identity in the 2020 election. Her feminist rhetoric should have been perfectly timed, with women's issues becoming more and more central to the news stories of this time, but it did not resonate. It may suggest that a woman candidate in particular has to modify the amount of times she uses feminist rhetoric and that it will resonate with only a portion of her audience—perhaps a small portion at that.

Although Gillibrand was not the only Democratic senator to call for Franken's resignation, she was the first, and she remains unapologetically anti-Franken. In a memorable *60 Minutes* profile, she said that although she still considers Franken a friend, "We just heard allegation after allegation, they were credible allegations; I believed the women,"[36] said Gillibrand. She became the political face of the #MeToo movement. Still, many believed that Franken was not given due process. After Franken resigned from the Senate, Pulitzer Prize–winning journalists Jodi Kantor and Megan Twohey, in a book about their investigation into the allegations against Harvey Weinstein and the consequences for the #MeToo movement, wrote that "more and more critics were complaining that men were becoming victims."[37]

Gillibrand failed to raise the money necessary to participate in the debates, a deciding factor for her. In a video message posted to her Twitter account, she shared her thoughts about her withdrawal from the race: "It is important to know when it's not your time, and to know how you can best serve your community and your country. I believe I can best serve by continuing to unite us to beat Donald Trump in 2020."[38] Her voice was raspy and her tone wistful.

Despite Gillibrand's position as a prominent Democratic senator, her campaign struggled. Running as a champion of feminism was not effective for Gillibrand. Despite her national profile, her feminist message did not break through in a field with six other women. With little money left and no place on the debate stage, she decided to drop out.

KIRSTEN GILLIBRAND'S PUBLIC SPEAKING

Kirsten Gillibrand is a polished, organized public speaker. She is lively and polished and appears well rehearsed and yet conversational and engaged in the moment.

Invention

Long before she ran for president, Kirsten Gillibrand has been invoking feminism in her speeches. She often draws from the lives of powerful women in her own family, underscoring that she has developed as a strong leader because of the strong women that came before her. Even in her launch speech for president, in front of the Trump International Hotel & Tower in New York City, Gillibrand asserted her theme of "Brave Wins" by providing evidence of Americans who have been brave. Within the examples she cites the women of America. She said:

> We are here today because we know that when we join together and fight for our values, brave wins. . . . The high school students who responded to unimaginable tragedy by organizing, marching and inspiring millions to end the epidemic of gun violence. That is brave. . . . The Dreamers who defiantly tell their stories and stand up for their right to call this country home. That is brave. . . . The sexual assault survivors who raise their voices against the powerful that tell them to stay silent. That is brave. . . . The millions of Americans who are speaking out against this Administration's cruelty toward women, Muslims, the LGBTQ community, and children at our border. That is brave. . . . And of course, the formerly well-behaved women who organized, ran for office, voted in record numbers and won in 2018. That too, is brave.[39]

Later in this speech, she recounted the mentorship and role modeling of her grandmother Polly:

> The fight ahead may seem daunting, but there is hope when we look down at our feet and see whose shoulders we stand on. We all have our heroes who inspire us in this struggle.
>
> My grandmother, Polly Noonan, was one of mine. She would be proud of us standing here today. She was larger than life. She was a firebrand and a Democratic organizer, who cursed like a sailor. She spent her life fighting for women to have a seat at the table.
>
> She never let anyone tell her that she couldn't or that she didn't belong. And she instilled that in me.

But more than anything else, my grandmother taught me that being brave doesn't just mean standing up for yourself, it means standing up for other people who need you and raising your voice on behalf of others who aren't being heard.

It's that core principle from my grandmother that has driven my life in public service. Over the years, I have learned that bravery means standing up to the powerful and summoning the courage to confront them head on.[40]

Kirsten Gillibrand served also as an advocate for the #MeToo movement, advocating on behalf of the women who accused powerful men of sexual harassment and abuse.

Disposition

Kirsten Gillibrand speaks about changing the leadership in the country and often disputes the current administration, stating how she would lead differently. She usually cites a portion of her resume to establish her credibility and assert that she is the right person for the job because she has been tested. An example of this can be found in her kickoff speech:

That's what I did when I first ran for Congress in a red red district that nobody thought I could win. Except for my mother—which tells you a lot about her. People told me: "It has more cows than Democrats—you just can't win!"

But, I took those long odds, and I won. And the next election, I won again—that time by a 24-point margin.

Why? Because I never forgot who I served.

That's why I stood up to greed and voted against the bank bailout that would leave taxpayers holding the bag. Even though I was warned it would end my career. It's why I stood up to corruption by making insider trading illegal for members of Congress. No one in our government should be lining their pockets as a public servant. It's why I stood up to callousness by demanding the 9/11 heroes be given the respect, compensation and health care they deserved.

And why I stood up to indifference and lies in the Pentagon, Congress, and colleges on behalf of survivors of sexual assault and harassment.

And it's why I stood up to bigotry and demanded the repeal of "Don't Ask Don't Tell," which was a corrosive and harmful policy that undermined our character and our national security.

And it's why I'm proud to have stood up to Donald Trump more than anyone else in the U.S. Senate.

Style

While many women running for political office can often be vague about their views on women's rights, Kirsten Gillibrand has made her views on women's equality the centerpiece of her political style. Her use of maternal family stories represents her most common stylistic device, and she uses the lessons of her grandmother and mother to argue for a new path for women, one where they are treated equally in all areas of life. Her own life as a mother while working as a senator provides her with myriad examples of how women have a challenging professional path because of the demands of both career and family. Another hallmark of her style is to describe her own marginalized treatment by often powerful men who have repeatedly remarked on her appearance in ways that men are rarely subjected.

Delivery

Kirsten Gillibrand's public speaking delivery is both polished and practiced and seemingly spontaneous. This is true because although she is clearly prepared, she will often interact with the audience and add to her original remarks with comments based on the feedback she is getting from the audience in the moment. Gillibrand favored tailored dresses during her presidential race, and always wore her blonde hair in a smooth bob. For example, in a speech she gave at the Iowa State Fair during the primary, she inserted, "So it's possible!,"[41] after she described how she beat her Republican opponent in a congressional race, explaining that if an opponent goes negative on a young mother with children, it just doesn't work. She often acts out the roles in her conversations as she speaks, enlivening her delivery by describing how she would ask senators across the aisle to support her positions. In this way, her delivery comes off as conversational and interactive. She is an experienced, articulate speaker and one who seems to revel in the storytelling nature of speaking as she recounts situations from her life as a child, impacted by feminist role models and her career as a congresswoman and senator.

Memoria

Kirsten Gillibrand's ability to master her material—her memoria—is impressive. Her ability to retain her messages for a fluid delivery is impressive. She sometimes speaks from prepared notes, or a teleprompter, and does so with smooth sophistication. She often delivers her speeches from memory, with equal finesse. She seems most comfortable when she moves around the stage, as she often did on the campaign trail during the presidential primary.

Obstacles to Her Presidential Bid

Kirsten Gillibrand's main rhetorical strategy was to advocate for the rights of women and girls; however, it seemed to resonate with only a small group of voters. The terribly crowded primary field made it hard for any candidate to stand out. Gillibrand's corny, somewhat childish slogan "Brave Wins" did not seem to catch fire. Choosing more clearly defined and concrete initiatives—ones that directly addressed the more salient issues facing voters who were seeking a broader, more populist message to counter Donald Trump's administration—perhaps would have resonated better. Also, the sense that Gillibrand is able to change her position to match the moment may have turned off voters. When she attacked Joe Biden in the debate over a decades-old op-ed piece, it came off as disingenuous and ineffective.

Flip-Flopping for Political Expediency

Early in her political career, Gillibrand held far more conservative positions on gun control and immigration. And, as a corporate lawyer, she represented a big tobacco company. These positions may have been seen as "flip-flops" to some voters who may have seen her as an opportunist.

Furthermore, Gillibrand was the first and most insistent of Democratic senators to ask for Al Franken to step down amid groping charges—although many felt he did not get due process. She also said publicly that Bill Clinton should have stepped down after the Monica Lewinsky scandal, a position that may not have been popular with other Democrats.

After her brief presidential bid in the primary, Kirsten Gillibrand returned to her work in the Senate, calling for the impeachment of President Donald Trump, and no doubt keeping her eye on future opportunities for a future presidential bid.

NOTES

1. Lizzo, "Good as Hell," https://www.google.com/search?q=come+on+dry+your+eyes+touh+the+sky+you+have+to+try&oq=come+on+dry+your+eyes+touh+the+sky+you+have+to+try&aqs=chrome.69i57j33.9746j0j7&sourceid=chrome&ie=UTF-8 (accessed January 9, 2019).

2. Gillibrand, Kirsten, campaign kickoff speech, March 24, 2019 https://www.c-span.org/video/?c4787454/user-clip-senator-kirsten-gillibrand-campaign-kickoff-speech (accessed January 9, 2019).

3. Gillibrand, Kirsten, *Off the Sidelines*, New York: Ballantine Books, 2014, 13.

4. https://www.nytimes.com/2018/09/05/theater/edie-falco-michael-mckean-the-true.html (accessed October 4, 2019).

5. Ibid., 28.

6. Ibid., 28.

7. Ibid., 15.

8. Ibid., 15.

9. Ibid., 15.

10. Ibid., 26.

11. Ibid., 35.

12. Ibid., 30.

13. Shapiro, Walter, "Who's Wearing the Pantsuit Now?" Elle, July 25, 2009, https://web.archive.org/web/20110307015848/http://www.elle.com/Life-Love/Society-Career-Power/Kirsten-Gillibrand (accessed October 4, 2019).

14. Gillibrand, Kirsten, 2020 Website, https://kirstengillibrand.com/issues/women-and-families/ (accessed October 9, 2019).

15. Ibid., 84.

16. Gillibrand, Kirsten, on *The Late Show with Stephen Colbert*, January 15, 2019. https://www.youtube.com/watch?v=q59SGJL3LMk (accessed July 16, 2019).

17. Gillibrand, Kirsten, presidential announcement speech, MSNBC, https://www.msnbc.com/weekends-with-alex-witt/watch/kirsten-gillibrand-officially-launches-presidential-campaign-in-new-york-1463959107560 (accessed October 9, 2019).

18. Ibid.

19. Ibid.

20. Ibid.

21. Gillibrand, Kirsten, MSNBC town hall, March 18, 2019, https://www.freep.com/story/news/politics/2019/03/18/kirsten-gillibrand-presidential-candidate-michigan-visit/3202981002/ (accessed January 9, 2019).

22. Ibid.

23. Ibid.

24. Ibid.

25. Ibid.

26. Ibid.

27. Gillibrand, Kirsten, Fox News town hall with Chris Wallace, https://www.foxnews.com/politics/fox-news-chris-wallace-calls-out-kirsten-gillibrand-for-impolite-jabs-at-network-during-townhall (accessed January 9, 2020).

28. Ibid.

29. Gillibrand, Kirsten, Iowa Hall of Fame event https://www.youtube.com/watch?v=vxn8JHhZNpw (accessed January 9, 2020).

30. Ibid.

31. Ibid.

32. Ibid.

33. "Kirsten Gillibrand's Clorox Comment the Debate Moment of the Night," Marie Claire, August 1, 2019 https://www.marieclaire.com/culture/a28571332/kirsten-gillibrand-clorox-debate/ (accessed January 13, 2020).

34. Kurtzelblen, Danielle, "Fact Check: Gillibrand Attacks Biden on 'deterioration of the family' Op/Ed," August 1, 2019, https://www.npr.org/2019/08/01/747122903/fact-check-gillibrand-attacks-biden-on-1981-deterioration-of-family-op-ed (accessed January 13, 2020).

35. Ibid.

36. Kirsten Gillibrand on *60 Minutes*, https://www.cbs.com/shows/60_minutes /video/ho59XwxupZ3LB_Hfbx2noTzsGyqerYP1/kirsten-gillibrand-the-60-minutes -interview/ (accessed October 9, 2019).

37. Kantor, Jodi, and Megan Twohey, She Said: Breaking the Sexual Harassment Story That Helped Ignite A Movement, New York: Penguin Press, 2019, 186.

38. Burns, Alexander, "Gillibrand Drops Out of 2020 Presidential Race," *The New York Times*, August 28, 2019, https://www.nytimes.com/2019/08/28/us/politics/ kirsten-gillibrand-2020-drop-out.html (accessed January 13, 2020).

39. Kirsten Gillibrand for President Website, https://kirstengillibrand.com/ (accessed March 26, 2020).

40. Ibid.

41. Gillibrand, Kirsten, Iowa Hall of Fame event https://www.youtube.com/watch ?v=vxn8JHhZNpw (accessed January 7, 2021).

Chapter 3

Kamala Harris

An Action-Oriented Advocate for the People

Kamala Harris recounts her upbringing often: the daughter of Shyamala Gopalan Harris, a single mother and scientist, who raised Kamala and her sister in a progressive fashion in Oakland, California. Although her mother raised the girls by herself, the influence of Donald Harris, her father and a renowned Stanford University economist, was strong; for him, education and activism were key family principles. Kamala would study political science and economics at Howard University, and then return to California for law school. Her path to political heights began to be shaped at Howard, as Juana Summers outlined in a National Public Radio piece that aired on August 2020. "In choosing Howard, regarded as one of the nation's premier historically Black educational institutions, Harris was immersing herself in Black culture and Black life," Summers said. "She pledged Alpha Kappa Alpha, the nation's oldest Black sorority, founded more than one hundred years ago at Howard. She attended protests against apartheid."[1]

And yet, despite the intensity of her commitment to civil rights, leadership, and activism, when Kamala Harris announced her presidential campaign in 2019 in Oakland, California, before a crowd of 20,000 supporters, her remarks started in way that embodied a California kind of cool. She was casual and smiling, acting as though the most natural thing in the world was for her to stand up in her hometown and let the world know that she was running for president. As her message continued, though, her casual, cool facade receded, and her presence on the stage—even the remarks she made—were also reminiscent of two previous trailblazers of color: Barack Obama and Shirley Chisholm.

Smiling broadly and clapping, the charismatic, comfortable communicator surveyed the crowd, waving "Kamala Harris For the People" signs and asked, "What's up, Oakland?" In response, the crowd started to shout "Kam-a-la!

Kam-a-la!"—chanting the name rhythmically and pronouncing it properly: Comma-la. Moved by their enthusiasm, Harris said, "OK! Thank you, thank you, thank you, thank you. Oh, my heart is full right now." She began by thanking Oakland mayor Libby Schaaff and then said, "Here we are. Well, let me tell you, I am so proud to be a daughter of Oakland, California."[2] In a presidential field dominated by white men, and in a field that has become dominated by white and male candidates, she was one of the few female and nonwhite contenders. Former president Barack Obama once called her "by far the best-looking attorney general in the country." (His point, it would seem, was that most of the rest of them were old white men, but it sounded sexist, and he apologized.)[3]

In her announcement speech, she also told of her upbringing in Oakland, how her parents met at the University of California, Berkeley, where they were active in the civil rights movement, and how they were "born half a world apart from each other. My father, Donald, came from Jamaica to study economics. My mother, Shyamala, came from India to study the science of fighting disease."[4] In citing her parents' origins, she echoed the language of Barack Obama's kingmaking speech at the 2004 Democratic National Convention when he described the unlikely partnering of his parents. He said, "Through hard work and perseverance my father got a scholarship to study in a magical place: America, which stood as a beacon of freedom and opportunity to so many who had come before. While studying here, my father met my mother. She was born in a town on the other side of the world, in Kansas."[5]

In a determined and inspired tone, Harris went on to explain that her parents came to the United States for more than education; they came to fulfill a dream. Quoting her mother, "Don't sit around and complain about things, do something."[6] And then she added, "Basically I think she was saying, 'You've got to get up and stand up and don't give up the fight'"—a line from a Bob Marley tune dating back to the 1970s. She laughed a full-throated but self-conscious laugh, diminishing the forcefulness of the statement and perhaps suggesting that she may have gone "over the top" by invoking the Marley lyric. As she began to outline her stance on key issues in the race and focus on specifics, her California cool and casual demeanor began to fade away, as though she took off her Chuck Taylor sneakers and switched to her polished pumps. Her tone changed, and her seriousness of purpose began to emerge.

Her slogan, "Kamala Harris For The People," came from her career as a prosecutor. The crowd at her presidential announcement speech roared when she said, "My whole life, I've only had one client: the people." This philosophy of service to the people is reminiscent of the "Unbought and Unbossed" mantra of Shirley Chisholm's 1972 campaign. Even the design and typography of Harris's signs, in all capital letters with her name in blue and "FOR THE PEOPLE" in red, was emblematic of 1970s style. She recounted her prosecutorial victories against banks' home foreclosures, gangs, guns, and drugs. She spoke against the Trump administration when she said, "And folks, on the subject of transnational gangs, let's be perfectly clear: The president's medieval vanity project is not going to stop them."[7]

Harris emphasized what would become an often-repeated line:

> We are at an inflection point in in the history of our nation. We are here because the American dream and our American democracy are under attack and on the line like never before. We are here at this moment in time because we must answer a fundamental question. Who are we? Who are we as Americans? So, let's answer that question. To the world. And each other. Right here. And, right now. America, we are better than this.

Throughout her speech, she used a "call-and-response" tactic to engage her audience. In a series of statements, she outlined assaults on U.S. institutions, racial minorities, immigrants, and public education, and abuses by banks. In response to each, her audience shouted, "That's not our America." Call-and-response style of public speaking began in African American culture and has a unique tradition in the United States, in particular, in black churches and in civil rights speeches.

Harris's "call" phrases included the following:

- When we have leaders who lie and bully and attack a free press and undermine our democratic institutions
- When white supremacists march and murder in Charlottesville or massacre innocent worshipers at a Pittsburgh synagogue
- When we have children in cages crying for their mothers and fathers, don't you dare call it border security, that's a human rights abuse
- When we have leaders who attack public schools and vilify public school teachers
- When bankers who crashed our economy get bonuses but workers who brought our country back can't even get a raise.[8]

She used this call-and-response method to great advantage, rallying her audience to participate in her speech, essentially denouncing the old America under the leadership of Donald Trump.

Harris had a breakout moment in the primary when she directed her remarks about desegregation and busing to Vice President Joseph R. Biden Jr. in the first Democratic debate in June 2019. It was early in the race, and most Americans were having trouble keeping track of the growing number of Democratic contenders. Kamala Harris personalized an issue that is important to many Americans, challenging Biden directly on the issues of race relations and segregation:

I'm going to now direct this at Vice President Biden. I do not believe you are
a racist. I agree with you when you commit yourself to the importance of finding common ground. I also believe . . . it's personal. It was actually hurtful to
hear you talk about the reputations of two United States senators who built their
reputations and career on the segregation of race in this country. It was not only
that, but you also worked with them to oppose busing. There was a little girl in
California who was part of the second class to integrate her public schools. She
was bused to school every day. That little girl was me. I will tell you that on this
subject it cannot be an intellectual debate among Democrats. We have to take it
seriously. We have to act swiftly. As attorney general of California, I was very
proud to put in place a requirement that all my special agents would wear body
cameras and keep those cameras on.[9]

Biden tried to defend himself, noting that his position was mischaracterized and that he in fact did not oppose busing. He tried to explain that he
did not want the federal government to get involved and instead wanted
individual states to handle it. However, regardless of what he said, he ended
abruptly, noting that "his time is up." (Metaphorically, Harris and other
Democratic hopefuls would readily agree that Biden's time on the national
political stage is or should be over.) Harris's performance in this debate, and
her willingness to pointedly ask Biden to defend himself, quickly gave her a
boost in the polls and greater name recognition, something urgent for candidates newer to the national stage. The busing issue, while a dramatic moment
during the debate, and a great press booster for Harris, when examined more
closely did not really call for such a dramatic stand from Harris, who had
not called for busing herself as a legislator. Her record on busing caused the
Biden campaign in the days following the debate to point out that Biden and
Harris were closer than it appeared at the debate on the subject of busing and
that Harris was looking to garner attention for herself during the debate. The
tactic worked since she was widely reported in the press the next day to have
stolen the show at that debate. Later in the campaign, once Biden had won
the nomination and was actively recruiting a female running mate, this debate
exchange would come up repeatedly as a potential reason why Biden would
not choose Harris as vice president.

Harris was actively taking on the front-runner, embodying the idea that
action beats inaction—a principle ingrained early in Kamala Harris's life
by her mother, who urged her to be a part of the solution. This would be the
high rhetorical mark of her campaign. While she gained significant press and
attention for her prosecutorial questioning of the former vice president—
adding to her credibility as an articulate, outspoken candidate—her positions seemed less clear to viewers. Taking on Biden was reminiscent of the
outspoken Shirley Chisholm, a fiery black leader who Harris came to know

at Rainbow Sign, a community center in Harris's Berkeley neighborhood. There, she would meet many people, besides Chisholm, who would help to stretch her imagination about what her future might look like. Fierce women role models, such as novelist Alice Walker, poet Maya Angelou, and singer Nina Simone, came to the forefront and made a strong impression on Harris.

GROWING UP IN OAKLAND AND INSPIRED BY HER ROLE MODEL SINGLE MOTHER

Kamala Harris was born on October 20, 1964, in California. Her mother, Shyamala Gopalan Harris, was an Indian immigrant and a breast cancer researcher at Canada's McGill University. Her father, Donald Harris, is a Stanford University economics professor who emigrated from Jamaica. Her parents met at graduate school at the University of California, Berkeley. In a 2019 interview, Kamala Harris said, "I am black and I am proud of it."[10] Harris recalls being steeped in her parents' activism. In speeches, she says she remembers being surrounded by "a bunch of adults who spent all their time marching and shouting—for justice!"[11]

Harris began kindergarten in Berkeley during the second year of the city's school desegregation busing program, which pioneered the extensive use of busing to bring racial balance to each of the city's public schools. A bus took Harris to a school which two years earlier had been 95 percent white.[12] Her parents divorced when she was seven, and her mother was granted custody of the children. After the divorce, when Harris was twelve, her mother moved with the children to Montreal, Quebec, Canada, where Shyamala accepted a position conducting breast cancer research and teaching at McGill University. Harris was enrolled at a neighborhood school for native French speakers, and despite being unhappy initially about the family's move to Canada, she made friends and performed well in school.

After graduating from high school, Harris majored in political science and economics at Howard University in Washington, DC, a place she found exceptionally welcoming and enriching. She writes, "This was the beauty of Howard. Every signal told students that we could be anything—that we were young, gifted and black, and we shouldn't let anything get in the way of our success."[13]

At Howard, she was elected to the liberal arts student council as freshman class representative and was a member of the debate team. After graduating, she went to California and earned her law degree from the University of California, Hastings College of the Law. She then began her rise in the California legal system, serving first as a prosecutor in the district attorney's office in Oakland's Alameda County, and then holding the same office in San

Francisco. After two terms as district attorney in San Francisco, she became state attorney general in 2010. She became the second African American woman and the first South Asian American to earn election to the U.S. Senate.

Harris likely came to the attention of many Americans during the televised hearings of the U.S. Senate Intelligence Committee's hearing on Russian interference in the 2016 presidential campaign. Harris stood out prior to the hearings as one of only three females and the only racial minority on the committee. Her communication style in the hearing—specifically, her strong, methodical responses to public interruptions by male colleagues—resonated strongly with many and gained her widespread media attention.

During the hearings, Harris was the only committee member to be interrupted—not once, but twice—during her allotted witness questioning time. On June 7, she was interrupted by committee chairman Richard Burr and Senator John McCain while questioning Deputy Attorney General Rod Rosenstein. Burr and McCain again interrupted Harris on June 13 during her questioning of Attorney General Jeffrey Sessions. Mainstream and social media took swift notice of these events, primarily speculating about why Harris was the only one to receive such treatment. In an essay in *Feminist Media Studies*,[14] Stephanie Norander argued that three distinct discursive framings of the interruptions reflect competing logics of difference and operate as sites of negotiation for the complex relationships among gender, race, and U.S. politics: gender imbalance, race and the need for discipline, and control of women of color.[15] We have seen these three themes emerge in the public profile of Michelle Obama, the first First Lady of color, who early in her husband's 2008 campaign for president was derided by the press as being an angry black woman. She has reflected on that characterization in her autobiography.

On January 21, 2019, during a Martin Luther King Jr. Day interview on *Good Morning America*, Harris—then U.S. senator from California— announced she was running for president in 2020. Her background as a prosecutor and district attorney became a key persuasive element of her presidential campaign. "I know the system from the inside out, so trust me when I say we have a problem with mass incarceration in America," she said. "Trust me when I say we have a problem with accountability. Trust me when I say we have to take the profit out of criminal justice."[16]

Harris no doubt chose this date to announce her candidacy with the significance of King's commitment to peace, racial equality, and justice in mind. One week after her announcement on early-morning television, Harris formally kicked off her campaign before an estimated 20,000 supporters at Frank Ogawa Plaza in Oakland, California—her beloved hometown. The huge crowd was a testament to the auspicious timing of the announcement and the interest in Harris as a presidential hopeful. Kamala Harris, Deval Patrick,

Cory Booker, Tulsi Gabbard, and Julián Castro brought much-needed racial diversity to the presidential race. Those elected to the U.S. presidency, except for Barack Obama in 2008, have exclusively been white men.

In the weeks following her announcement, Harris remained near the top of the Democratic polls, despite the brouhaha that followed a February 2019 interview, when she admitted to smoking marijuana, and another that occurred in June, when an animal rights activist confronted her onstage at a political event. By the next Martin Luther King Jr. Day, she had suspended her presidential campaign, and yet her short bid made an impact on the presidential race of 2020.

THE RHETORIC OF KAMALA HARRIS'S PRESIDENTIAL CAMPAIGN THROUGH SPEECHES AND NOTABLE DISCOURSE

Harris stood out as one of the top performers of the first Democratic primary debate in late June, garnering headlines for taking former vice president Biden to task over his history of opposing federal busing for school integration. She spoke calmly but emotionally about a "little girl in California" who was bused to school every day as part of an integration plan in Berkeley—a plan that Biden had worked to stop as a U.S. senator. "That little girl was me," she said. Furthermore, Biden had boasted about his ability to work well with political opponents, citing his connection to senators known for their racist views. She told Biden it was "hurtful to hear you talk about the reputations of two United States senators who built their reputations and career on the segregation of race in this country."[17] This debate performance was heavily covered by the press and it showcased Harris's telegenic, charismatic qualities as well as her debating acumen, which so often includes well-prepared attack lines and withering interrogation. Her anecdote about her experience riding the bus to school was the clear headline-grabber of the evening. Her success in the first debate was undeniable: she took well-crafted, quotable statements, and offered a passionate, well-timed delivery. It was hard to stand out in the crowded field, but Harris did, even injecting humor into a thoughtful statement about the infighting happening during the debate.

"America does not want to witness a food fight," she said. "They want to know how we're going to put food on their table." And, "the rules have been written in the favor of the people who have the most and not in favor of the people who work the most."[18] However, the wave of popularity for Harris's presidential bid did not last long. Harris found herself a target of attacks during the debate the following month, with Biden and the rest criticizing her health care plan and aspects of her record as California attorney general.

In June, she gave a speech at the Iowa Hall of Fame event, and she began with a casual, colloquial "What's up, Iowa?!" She told a story about her first trip to the state and how a group of teachers pointedly asked her what she planned to do to make pay for teachers more equitable. "And it was because of the conversation that we had that as my first policy proposal," she said. "I am prepared to make the first federal investment in the history of our country in closing that teacher pay gap." She went on to talk about other initiatives that she planned to spearhead as president, such as health care and increasing the minimum wage. As so often was the case with her presidential speeches, she went into her biography, describing herself as "a daughter of the civil rights movement." She said, "In fact, our mother was all of five feet tall, but if you had ever met her, you would have thought she was seven feet tall. And my mother was the kind of person who, if you ever came home complaining about something, the first thing she'd do—she might put a hand on a hip—she'd look at you and she'd say, 'So what are you gonna do about it?' So I decided to run for president of the United States."

She also described her career as a prosecutor. "I prosecuted those who would prey on the most vulnerable: murderers and rapists. I prosecuted banks. I prosecuted big pharmaceutical companies who were preying on the most vulnerable and consumers. I prosecuted the big banks and for-profit colleges who are defrauding homeowners and consumers. And I'm gonna tell you somebody else who has defrauded the American people: Donald Trump."[19] She concluded her speech by calling out all the types of fraud she argues Donald Trump has committed: health care fraud, tax fraud, securities fraud, and identity fraud. "So I'm here to ask for your support. I'm here to support because I am prepared to make the case for America and to prosecute the case against Donald Trump!" In Iowa, Kamala Harris began to use the phrase "Dude gotta go!" in reference to Donald Trump.[20]

Kamala Harris is a notably articulate and effective public speaker, with a comfortable, conversational, casual style. She has a lot of charisma, star power, and energy, often running on to the stage to the music of "My Shot" from the Broadway show *Hamilton*. The lyrics capture her competitive spirit:

I am not throwing away my shot
I am not throwing away my shot.[21]

She obviously did not fall into the trap of not taking advantage of a good opportunity that many politicians do when it comes to responses to pointed press questions. A good example of her sophisticated handling of communication exchanges was her response to questions from CNN's Kyung Lah after President Donald Trump fired off racist tweets attacking four Democratic congresswomen. Harris said Donald Trump's tweets were "un-American" and "unbecoming of the president of the United States. I think it defiles the office of president of the United States." She continued: "It's one thing to hear it in a schoolyard, or on the street. It's another thing to hear that from the President of the United States. . . . The president of the United States has a very powerful, powerful voice, and [a powerful] tool, which is that microphone. . . . The strength of the office should be to lift people up and not beat them down. But this president, I guess, thinks he becomes stronger by those who he pushes down. Well, that's not reflective of who we are as a nation. It is not reflective of the values we have as Americans."

She went on to say, "I have said it many times. This president purposely, I believe, distracts, and attempts to distract, by flame throwing, because the reality of it is, he has done nothing to help working families in America."[22]

Words: Is policy relevant and how will it impact real people? Not is it a beautiful sonnet? Otherwise it is just an idea.

She is not an ideologue.

Her three litmus test questions, she says, or the "litmus tests of the relevancy of policy," are as follows:

1. Does it help a substantial number of people?
2. How does it affect children?
3. How long will it take?

> The significance of the passage of time . . . all those who knew the importance of getting that case there (Brown v Board of education) . . . all the people had to be patient to some extent knowing that they had to build up precedent. It was decided in May, 1954 and everyone is sitting around (cha ching cha ching—) with glasses of chardonnay and champagne saying: "Oh this is lovely we won . . ." but not until twenty years later did it reach the streets of Berkeley, CA.[23]

As Harris's campaign lost the initial momentum it experienced during the debate, she kept stressing the theme with which she rolled out her campaign: That she is "fighting for justice." However, she also began to question whether Americans were ready to elect a woman of color as president. She approached this by playing off the phrase "the elephant in the room"—meaning an obvious question or issue that no one wants to address—by referring to "the donkey in the room."[24] In Iowa in October 2019, she wondered aloud, "Is America ready for that? Are they ready for a woman of color to be president?"

As Harris's numbers continued to spiral downward in late summer 2019, she also began to revisit a rhetorical trope that she used to demonstrate she is a tough competitor, perhaps to show that she could beat Donald Trump. When she ran for attorney general, she trailed behind Steve Cooley, a moderate Republican with deep roots in Southern California. "Harris, nearly two decades younger and the daughter of immigrants from India and Jamaica, looked like nobody who held the state's top law enforcement office before. Harris won the race with a late surge: she capitalized on a mistake by her opponent. She outworked him in the closing stretch. And she persuaded Californians to take a chance on a new kind of attorney general."[25]

The attempt for female candidates to show toughness is not new. Geraldine Ferraro did it in 1984 as a vice presidential candidate, when she used the slogan "Finally, A Tough Democrat."[26] Harris gained a reputation for her tough rhetoric from her pointed questioning of Brett Kavanaugh during his U.S. Supreme Court nomination hearings and U.S. attorney general William Barr during hearings into Russian interference in the 2016 election. She continued this tough talk into her presidential race, though she augmented it with pieces of her biography and her personal life, disclosing characteristics that would endear her to voters, something female candidates in particular struggle to do successfully. In their 2013 article Monica C. Schneider and Angela L. Bos point out that one explanation for the dearth of women in elected office is that voters stereotype candidates based on their gender. In particular, they note that most voters do not believe that women in general are tough enough to handle the rough challenges that confront elected officials.[27]

Media Frames

One of the media frames that continued to surface about Harris were her previous statements on health care. She sometimes seemed to support Bernie Sanders's call for "Medicare for All," and yet at other times rejected aspects of the plan unpopular with moderate voters, such as tax increases on some middle-class families. This lack of clarity raised question marks in the minds of voters who were impressed with her performance but questioned her actual positions.

Harris's rhetoric as a presidential contender suggested that she wanted to underscore her fighting, prosecutor background, and call on voters of America to realize that if there is going to be change, there must be new leadership. She said:

> We are at an inflection point in in the history of our nation. We are here because the American dream and our American democracy are under attack and on the line like never before. We are here at this moment in time because we must answer a fundamental question. Who are we? Who are we as Americans?

> So, let's answer that question. To the world. And each other. Right here. And, right now.

> America, we are better than this.[28]

The media was more likely to cast her as the "female Obama," a "cool aunt" persona that could even be seen in a satirical *Saturday Night Live* skit. Obama's coolheaded personality comes through in Maya Rudolph's portrayal of Harris in the SNL send-up of the 2020 Democratic debate. As Harris, Rudolph winks at the camera as she says, "Mama Need a GIF." Later in the skit she says, "There have been two Black women elected to the Senate, and that second woman"—as she puts on a cowboy hat—"It. Me."[29]

The media also paid attention to comments and questions about Harris's black identity.

On *The Breakfast Club* radio show, hosts DJ Envy and Charlamagne Tha God asked Harris about that. "Harris pushed back. 'I'm black, and I'm proud of being black. I was born black. I will die black. I'm not going to make excuses for anybody because they don't understand.'"[30] She went on to criticize those who question her racial identity. "I think they don't understand who black people are," Harris said. "I'm not going to spend my time trying to educate people about who black people are. Because right now, frankly, I'm focused on, for example, an initiative that I have that is called the LIFT Act that is about lifting folks out of poverty."[31]

KAMALA HARRIS'S PUBLIC SPEAKING

Kamala Harris is a passionate, biographical speaker who appears utterly at ease in front of a camera and on the campaign trail interacting with voters. She intertwines tough rhetoric with warm, conversational disclosures of her biography.

Invention

Many of the topics of Harris's public speaking mention the strong role model she found in her mother. She rarely mentions her father, except in relationship to her mother, and she makes it clear that her mother is the parent who shaped her and gave her the drive to be politically active. A typical example of this occurs in a speech she gave at a house party in Des Moines, Iowa, where she spoke of her mother's influence:

> "She was one of the very few women of color in science," Harris said. "When I decided to run, she said, 'Honey, you watch out for what's going to happen, because there are still certain myths about what women can do and cannot do, in spite of the fact of what women *actually* do in life.' And she said, 'Two of those myths are that women can do certain things but not necessarily be in charge of your security or your money.' In spite of the fact that, Who is the

lioness protecting those cubs at all costs? Who is it who is invariably sitting at that kitchen table in the middle of the night trying to figure out how to get those bills paid?"[32]

Other themes found in her speaking include Medicare for All, economic relief, and recovery, asking in her stump speech what wakes the American people at 3:00 a.m.? She would argue that is not ideological mudslinging but "practical concerns: holding down a job, getting through a health crisis, weathering hurricanes and tornadoes."[33]

Disposition

Kamala Harris often organizes her speeches by offering a part of her biography, referencing her life growing up and the lessons she learned from her activist parents. As the 2020 primary election process went on, Harris argued more forcefully that Donald Trump needs to be replaced and she was the one to replace him. In a speech at the 2019 Iowa Democratic Party's Liberty and Justice Celebration, Harris intertwined her experience as a prosecutor with the reasons she was the best candidate to defeat Donald Trump.

Kamala Harris would use those reasons to organize the body of her speeches and use repetition of key phrases to hammer home her major points. Representative of the way she began to organize her arguments was her repeated use of the phrase "We are here to end that national nightmare of Donald Trump." She often used this phrase in her primary speeches and she also used it at the "Liberty and Justice" fundraising event. She began to use "We have to fight" and "For the people" as repetitive stances. She forcefully declared what it would take "to win." She would use the phrase repeatedly. "To win: We have to be focused on tomorrow." Again she would say, "To win: We are going to need a nominee on that stage with Donald Trump who can go toe to toe with Donald Trump, and Iowa, you are looking at her." She offered the main reason her debate skills are strong by saying, "I've spent my career as a prosecutor, and I've only had one client in my career, and that's the people. I've started my career fighting for the people and the first time I walked into a courtroom I spoke five words: Kamala Harris for the people."[34]

Style

Kamala Harris's typical use of language in her speeches—her rhetorical style—is dynamic and contemporary. She is completely accessible as a public figure, often uses casual words like "hey" and "wow," and completely at ease communicating in casual settings, such as when she received a phone call from President-elect Joe Biden while walking in casual running clothes and saying, "We did it!" much as a coach at a high school basketball game would commend her team. The most significant aspect of Harris's style is her relaxed, California cool colloquiality. While some politicians may have a stiff and proper air given the gravity of their work, Harris has a disarming connection with her communicators—whether it is Brett Kavanaugh, Joe Biden, or the American people. She speaks as though she is sitting in your home, at your kitchen table, having a conversation, likely in her beloved "Chucks" sneakers over a cup of coffee. Her Berkeley upbringing is evident in her approach to discuss and deliberate issues of the country as if they are those of a small town—casual, intimate, and without airs. Smart, stylish Kamala Harris cuts an impressive figure as a modern politician who grew up in a progressive area of California and who had a strong role model in her mother. While she often spoke about her activist parents, and her desire to strengthen the lives of the marginalized, she could not lay claim to the same "catalyst for change" type of rhetoric that Shirley Chisholm embodied. And yet, her ambitious career and political path is one pointed to service and justice, two themes that arise often in both Harris's and Chisholm's rhetoric.

Delivery

Kamala Harris delivers her speeches with youthful vigor, energy, polish, and charisma. She seems to truly enjoy public speaking, a skill she honed as a member of her debate club in high school. Her appearance is striking, her hair beautifully styled, and she favors monochromatic tailored pantsuits over skirted suits. She has a dignified yet approachable demeanor, and she often smiles and gestures, appearing comfortable moving around as she speaks, using her hands to gesticulate and underscore her points. She can be the affable, fun politician, but she quickly grows serious and pointed when she is making a particular statement of import or asking a deliberate question. For example, at one debate she said, "Donald Trump came in making a whole lot of promises to working people that he did not keep. He said he was going to help farmers. He said he was going to help autoworkers."[35] She seems to be a naturally gifted speaker, in full command of her speech.

Memoria

Harris's command of her material—her memoria—is impressive. She is a comfortable, relaxed, almost always smiling and composed speaker. An eloquent, commanding, and natural speaker, she works the crowd with a casual kind of back-and-forth as though she has nothing to worry about. Her voice has a nasal quality to it, and she has a habit of laughing after a forceful statement, which takes away from the potency of the statement. For example, when she repeats "Kamala Harris For the People," she chuckles a bit, as though it is a humorous statement, which, I think most people would agree it is not. Although humor is a good thing in general, it is not effective when it appears to undercut a speaker's message.

Obstacles to Her Presidential Bid

An inability to articulate a consistent rationale for Harris's candidacy was a major failing throughout her campaign. Her critics argue that missteps, such as ignoring Iowa and New Hampshire in early critical months, "suggested to voters that she was unprepared for the presidency, lending credence to arguments questioning her electability."[36] She was unable to draw large audiences, despite her charisma and credentials. "She was stuck in the mid-single digits in most national polls and drew modest crowds."[37]

She had inconsistent performances. In the first debate, she was great, and in subsequent debates, not memorable at all. She was also described as arrogant in the press.[38]

And yet, Carol Moseley Braun, the only other living black woman to have run for president, noted that Harris seemed to have advantages in 2020 that were not afforded to her when she ran in 2004. "There are clear signs of progress in recruitment and the public discussion of diverse leadership."[39]

Harris did not have one unifying theme for her presidential campaign. Her visual rhetoric of "Kamala Harris For The People" was very strong, although her verbal messages were varied and inconsistent. From the initial theme of "speaking truth," her campaign moved to "prosecuting the case against Donald Trump," the "3 a.m. call," and finally "Justice is on the ballot." She also started to say "Dude's Gotta Go" in referring to Trump, yet another theme/message. These many messages suggest that her campaign was searching for the one that would resonate and bring her poll numbers back up to where they were after the first debate, when she took on Joe Biden over school busing. But they never did rebound. Two months before the Iowa caucus even took place, Harris withdrew her name from the presidential race and returned to her work in the Senate.

When Harris dropped out of race, she tweeted, "To my supporters, it is with deep regret—but also with deep gratitude—that I am suspending my campaign today. But I want to be clear with you: I will keep fighting every day for what this campaign has been about. Justice for the people. All the people. I've taken stock and looked at this from every angle, and over the last few days have come to one of the hardest decisions of my life. My campaign for president simply doesn't have the financial resources we need to continue."[40] In a video explaining her decision to drop out, Harris said, "I'm not a billionaire. I can't fund my own campaign. . . . And as the campaign has gone on, it has become harder and harder to raise the money we need to compete. In good faith, I can't tell you, my supporters and volunteers, that I have a path forward if I don't believe I do."

AFTER HER PRESIDENTIAL BID

Harris reemerged onto the national stage during the height of the Covid-19 crisis in the United States. She touted the efficient leadership in her state of California, and rebuked President Trump for his focus on himself instead of the crises, asserting that "this guy just doesn't understand his job."[41] She called on President Trump to "meet the needs of the moment." She also cited California leaders as extraordinary, including San Francisco mayor London Breed who, according to Harris, was "the first mayor in the country to call for a stay-at-home order."[42]

Vice Presidential Candidate

In a selection process that at time felt like a reality television dating program, Democratic nominee Joe Biden, intent on selecting a woman, interviewed as many as a dozen women for the coveted job as his vice presidential running mate. Kamala Harris was consistently at the top of the list. Eventually, she was chosen for many of the reasons that any running mate is chosen. Harris is from a large, important state, she has experience in elected office, most recently as a U.S. senator, and she has a national profile, mostly seared in voters' minds from her bid for the presidency. She is also someone Biden felt he could work well with and someone who would be qualified and ready to serve as president immediately, if needed.

More important, however, was what we know in rhetoric as "kairos"—the concept of taking action at the proper or optimal time. Harris's selection was about more than her identity as a black woman; it was also about the racial unrest that has been part of America's history since slavery, the civil rights movement of the 1960s, and of course, the civil unrest brought on by the deaths of Breonna Taylor and George Floyd. The choice of Kamala Harris signaled that the white male club of national politics may be over for good: In an America that is now more diverse than ever, women are running for political office in greater numbers. Her selection as vice president marked a hopeful new beginning for women in politics during a time in the United States when the Covid-19 pandemic was raging, social unrest was high, and the unemployment rate was soaring. Furthermore, as Election Day neared, the country learned that President Donald Trump and First Lady Melania Trump had tested positive for Covid-19. This "October Surprise" heightened interest in the qualifications of both Vice President Mike Pence and Senator Kamala Harris, since both Donald Trump, ill with Covid-19, and Joe Biden, about to turn seventy-eight, made the vibrancy, qualifications, and rhetoric of the vice presidential candidates that much more pertinent. Kamala Harris's bid for the presidency proved especially fruitful for her: had she not entered the national conversation as a presidential candidate who promised to stop Donald Trump and work "for the people," it is unlikely she would have been chosen as the vice presidential candidate. Indeed, Kamala Harris has changed presidential politics in the United States forever. She is the first woman to serve as vice president, and she has proven that when women run, women win—perhaps not the office they are seeking at the time—but they may win in a way that inches forward Madam President in the future more dramatically than any woman who has run for president previously.

NOTES

1. Juana Summers, "Howard University Shaped Kamala Harris' Path to Political Heights," NPR, August 19, 2020. https://www.npr.org/2020/08/19/903716274/howard -university-shaped-kamala-harris-path-to-political-heights (accessed August 25, 2020).

2. Sen. Kamala Harris Presidential Campaign Announcement, January 27, 2019, https://www.youtube.com/watch?v=m4ecapNBaXU (accessed July 31, 2019).

3. Dana Goodyear, "Kamala Harris Makes Her Case," *The New Yorker*, July 15, 2019, https://www.newyorker.com/magazine/2019/07/22/kamala-harris-makes-her -case (accessed April 2, 2020).

4. Ibid.

5. Barack Obama, 2004 Democratic National Convention Speech, PBS, https:// www.pbs.org/newshour/show/barack-obamas-keynote-address-at-the-2004-demo- cratic-national-convention (accessed August 21, 2020).

6. Kamala Harris Presidential Announcement Speech transcript, Carrie Chapman Catt Center, Iowa State University, https://awpc.cattcenter.iastate.edu/2019/02/28/pres- idential-campaign-announcement-january-28-2019/ (accessed September 18, 2020).

7. Sen. Kamala Harris Presidential Campaign Announcement, January 27, 2019, https://www.youtube.com/watch?v=m4ecapNBaXU (accessed July 31, 2019).

8. Ibid.

9. Edith Honan, "'That little girl was me': Kamala Harris and Biden Spar Over Desegregation at Debate," ABC News, June 27, 2019, *https://abcnews.go .com/Politics/girl-senator-harris-vice-president-biden-spar-desegregation/story?id =64007842* (accessed February 1, 2021).

10. Molly Ball, "Finding Kamala Harris: Emphatic But Elusive, the Candidate Searches for her Place in the Democratic Field," TIME, October 14, 2019, 33.

11. Ibid.

12. Saranac Hale Spencer, "Sen. Harris Didn't 'Lie' About Integration," Factcheck .org., July 13, 2018.

13. Kamala Harris, *The Truths We Hold: An American Journey*, New York: Penguin, 2019, 22.

14. Stephanie Norander (2017), "Kamala Harris and the interruptions heard around the internet," *Feminist Media Studies*, 17:6, 1104–1107, DOI: 10.1080/14680777.2017.1380427.

15. Ibid.

16. Astead W. Herndon, "Harris says 'Trust Me' On Need for Criminal Justice Reform," *The New York Times*, September 10, 2019, A16.

17. Molly Ball, "The Strife of the Party: The Democrats' debate will shape America's Future," TIME, August 5, 2020, 21.

18. Ellie Bufkin, "Kamala Harris: That Little Girl Was Me," *Washington Examiner*, June 27, 2019, https://www.washingtonexaminer.com/news/kamala-harris -says-she-was-a-victim-of-bidens-racial-policies (accessed March 30, 2020).

19. Ibid.

20. Shane Goldmacher, "In Iowa, a Bid to Make Up for Lost Time," *The New York Times*, August 12, 2019, A10.

21. https://www.lyrics.com/lyric/32212242/Lin-Manuel+Miranda/Alexander +Hamilton.

22. CNN's Kyung Lah interview, July 16, 2019. https://www.youtube.com/watch ?v=OTOTnWJe6LE (accessed July 17, 2019).

23. The Daily with Michael Barbaro, July 31, 2019 (transcribed from podcast).

24. Christopher Cadelago, "How Harris Went from 'Female Obama' to Fifth Place, *Politico*, November 5, 2019, https://www.politico.com/magazine/story/2019 /11/05/how-kamala-harris-went-from-female-obama-to-fifth-place-229901 (accessed March 29, 2020).

25. Ibid.

26. Douglas Martin, "She Ended the Men's Club in National Politics," *The New York Times*, March 26, 2011, https://www.nytimes.com/2011/03/27/us/politics /27geraldine-ferraro.html (accessed March 27, 2020).

27. Monica C. Schneider, and Bos, A.L. (2014), Measuring Stereotypes of Female Politicians. *Political Psychology*, 35: 245-266. doi:10.1111/pops.12040.

28. Sen. Kamala Harris Presidential Campaign Announcement, January 27, 2019, https://www.youtube.com/watch?v=m4ecapNBaXU (accessed July 31, 2019).

29. 2020 Democratic Debate—*Saturday Night Live*, YouTube video, accessed April 7, 2020.

30. Eugene Scott, "Why Some African Americans are Questioning Kamala Harris's Blackness," *The Washington Post*, June 28, 2019, https://www.washington-post.com/politics/2019/02/14/why-some-african-americans-are-questioning-kamala -harriss-blackness/ (accessed April 8, 2020).

31. Ibid.

32. Goodyear, "Kamala Harris Makes Her Case."

33. Ball, "Finding Kamala Harris."

34. Kamala Harris, 2019 Liberty and Justice Celebration, Iowa, C-Span Archives, https://www.c-span.org/video/?c4827095/user-clip-sen-kamala-harris-2019-liberty -justice-dinner-des-moines-iowa (accessed April 16, 2020).

35. Tankersley, Jim and Ben Casselman, "Trade War and Axes: Where Rivals May Hit Trump on the Economy," *The New York Times*, August 2, 2019, A17.

36. Lisa Lerer and Jennifer Medina, "The Burdens of Black Women in Politics," *The New York Times*, December 9, 2019, A11.

37. Ball, "Finding Kamala Harris." *TIME*, October 14, 2019, 32.

38. Astead W. Herndon, "Why Kamala Harris Is Not Clamoring To Be Joe Biden's Running Mate," *The New York Times*, May 11, 2020, https://www.nytimes .com/2020/05/11/us/politics/kamala-harris-biden-vp.html?searchResultPosition=1 (accessed May 15, 2020).

39. Ibid.

40. https://www.politico.com/news/2019/12/03/kamala-harris-drops-out-out-of -presidential-race-074902.

41. Senator Harris: This Guy Just Doesn't Understand His Job, MSNBC, April 2, 2020.

42. Senator Harris: 'Let's Meet The Needs Of The Moment' | Deadline | MSNBC, April 1, 2020.

Chapter 4

Amy Klobuchar

A Pragmatic Approach to Presidential Leadership

As the returns for the New Hampshire primary in February came in, Minnesota senator Amy Klobuchar could see that her nascent presidential campaign was breaking through, and that she was having a good showing. The fiscally moderate Democrat, who opposed "Medicare for All" and free college, jubilantly declared, "I can promise you this: When I am behind that desk, I will take responsibility instead of passing it on." Accusing the president of blaming others "for everything that goes wrong," she added, "I will reach across the aisle and work with Americans in good faith instead of picking fights. I will bring this country together."[1]

This practical can-do message was consistent with her industrious, conciliatory work in the Senate. But when the votes were counted, Amy Klobuchar had finished third—behind well-known Vermont senator Bernie Sanders and a national newcomer Pete Buttigeig, the eloquent and earnest former South Bend, Indiana, mayor. While a third-place finish has historically been a letdown to most politicians in the New Hampshire primaries of the past, for Klobuchar—the gritty, razor-sharp Midwestern senator with a message of centrist unity and experience—third place must have felt like first. Indeed, her remarks made it sound as though she had won.

How Klobuchar declared victory—with a third-place finish—was reminiscent of Bill Clinton's declaration that he was "the Comeback Kid" in 1992 when he came in second in New Hampshire to Paul Tsongas. Both of these seasoned politicians—Clinton in 1992 and Klobuchar in 2019—were clearly surprised and euphoric over their finishes. They took to the podium with equal parts vigor and a sense of victory, declaring, in essence, that their primary showings were the beginning of something big. Grinning from ear to ear, Klobuchar declared, "Thank you, New Hampshire! We love you, New

Hampshire! Hello, America. I'm Amy Klobuchar and I will beat Donald Trump!"[2] The audience roared: "Beat Trump. Beat Trump!"[3]

That down-to-earth, appealing tendency to introduce herself with a humble "I'm Amy Klobuchar" is a trademark of the senator, who does not take for granted that anyone knows her. After thanking her family—husband John and daughter Abigail—along with her staff and volunteers, she underscored the fundamental reason for her campaign: to unify the country. She reiterated one of the themes that became a way to show that it is time for someone like her to lead: "In a democracy, it is not about the loudest voice or the biggest bank account. It is about the best ideas and about the person who can turn those ideas into action."[4]

She was painting a picture for the voters that she is resilient and tough, and that she came from humble and hardworking roots. Her stories drew them in. She recounted how her "grandpa worked fifteen hundred feet underground in the mines in northern Minnesota. He never graduated from high school because his parents were sick, he had nine brothers and sisters, and he had to help raise them. Every day he would go down in that cage in that mine, carrying a lunch bucket that my grandma would pack. His youngest sister, Hannah, was only eight years old when they put her in an orphanage. He vowed after his parents died that he would go and get her. Two years later, he borrowed a car, he went to Duluth, and he brought her home."[5]

She tenderly told how her grandma saved money in a coffee can in the basement to send her dad to a two-year community college, and how her mom was a second-grade teacher who taught until she was seventy years old. To this day, Klobuchar recounted, she meets former students of her mother who tell her that her mother was their favorite teacher. While proud that her mother taught until she was seventy, Klobuchar told her listeners how she hopes they will be able to retire when they are younger than that.

She also let voters know that she didn't come from a perfect family. She described her father's painful battle with alcoholism, the breakup of her parents' marriage, and the challenges she faced when her only child, a daughter, Abigail was born and had to stay in intensive care. Having been sent home from the hospital when she could have benefited from a few more days of hospital care, she was inspired to run for office to change the way maternal care is offered in the United States. These remarkably personal stories were in so many ways the unremarkable stories many voters have experienced themselves, and they were relatable. They showed Amy Klobuchar's toughness, grit, resiliency, and connection to the middle class. They showed that her life is so much like the lives led by Americans everywhere.

"That's how I do my work," Klobuchar added. She recalled a comment earlier that evening from her friend and fellow presidential candidate Elizabeth Warren, U.S. senator from Massachusetts: "People told me, just like they told her, that they didn't think a woman could be elected. In my case, it was elected to the U.S. Senate. No woman had ever done it before."

> But I came back, I defied expectations, and I won. I have done it over and over again in the reddest of red districts and the bluest of blue districts. When I got to the U.S. Senate, people told me, "It's so hard to get things done." Well, in that gridlock of Washington, D.C., I have passed over 100 bills as a lead Democrat, because I did not give up.[6]

This story of her trailblazing efforts, on the campaign trail and in Congress, provides evidence that tenacity and persistence can defy the odds. In a campaign where there was doubt about who could beat incumbent Donald Trump, Klobuchar was trying to prove that she could, noting that she has surprised naysayers and beat Republicans in solidly red districts. Undeniably, Klobuchar's history of electoral wins is impressive. She won all three of her Senate elections by more than twenty percentage points and in 2018 she carried fifty-one of Minnesota's eighth-seven counties.

She repeatedly told a story about Franklin Delano Roosevelt, whose body, after his death, was put on a train that traveled through the countryside from Warm Springs, Georgia, to Washington, DC, and then to Hyde Park, New York:

> People would spontaneously stand next to those rail tracks to show their respect. The story goes that one guy was standing there sobbing. Regular guy. Had his hat across his chest. This reporter says to him, "Sir, did you know President Roosevelt? Do you mind me asking, did you know him?" And the guy says, "No, I didn't know President Roosevelt, but he knew me. He knew me."

She promised to restore the kind of sacred trust the man was talking about and she promised to bring empathy back to the White House.

With the front-runner status of former vice president Joseph R. Biden Jr. in question after the Iowa caucus and New Hampshire primary, Amy Klobuchar, the very relatable senator, who may remind you of your next-door neighbor, emerged in so many ways as a standard-bearer for the Democratic center. The word she so often evokes to describe her political work—grit—seemed especially fitting after her gritty showing in the New Hampshire primary. Her persuasive points are often focused on what she has done—sponsored or cosponsored more than 100 bills that became law—and worked across the aisle. According to the findings of a study from the Center for Effective Lawmaking at Vanderbilt University, she is the most productive senator in the Democratic field of presidential candidates. (The 2019 study named Klobuchar and Iowa senator Chuck Grassley the most effective senators in the 115th Congress, based on metrics that take into account the number of bills a legislator sponsors, how far each of those bills advances through the legislative process, and its significance.[7]

It is likely that Klobuchar first came to the attention of many Americans during the Brett Kavanaugh Supreme Court confirmation hearings. The hearing—in which Kavanaugh was defending himself against allegations of sexual assault—thrust Klobuchar into the national spotlight. Klobuchar began by mentioning the challenges with alcoholism faced by her father and proceeded to ask Kavanaugh, in a respectful and serious manner, whether he had ever used so much alcohol that he could not remember what had happened during the time he had been drinking.

Kavanaugh, who had previously expressed appreciation for the way Klobuchar asked probing but respectful questions earlier in the hearings, responded that his answer was no. He then gratuitously asked, more in the style of a political opponent than a judge considering a case, whether Klobuchar had ever drunk so much she could not remember what she did at the time. Kavanaugh then repeated his attack line against Klobuchar a second time, after which she responded calmly and professionally by repeating her question.

The exchange:

Klobuchar: "You're saying there's never been a case where you drank so much that you didn't remember what happened the night before or part of what happened?"
Kavanaugh: "If you're asking about blackout. I don't know—have you?"
Klobuchar: "Could you answer the question, Judge? . . . So, that's not what happened, is that your answer?"
Kavanaugh: "Yeah, and I'm curious if you have."
Klobuchar: "I have no drinking problem, judge."
Kavanaugh: "Nor do I."
Klobuchar: "OK. Thank you."

In this transcript from the Kavanaugh hearing, many Americans got a glimpse of how a steady, strong communicator, and seasoned politician—Klobuchar—can defuse the anger and exert calm control over a potentially volatile situation. That Kavanaugh later apologized to Klobuchar is evidence that she was the strong one, and the person who could avert a blowup, something that has become all too common in national discourse.

Klobuchar's focused exchange with Kavanaugh showed that she was a tough questioner. But her toughness really came into view when she went on the offensive against Michael Bloomberg, the former mayor of New York City, during the televised Democratic debate in late February 2020. "I think we need someone different than Donald Trump. I don't think people look at Donald Trump and think, 'We need someone richer in the White House.'"[8] Later in the debate, Pete Buttigieg accused her of not knowing the name of the president of Mexico. The two dismissed each other's experience as irrelevant to governing, Klobuchar saying that Buttigieg hasn't been "in the arena" and pointing to her winning record as proof that she has the resume to win the White House. Buttigieg all but called Klobuchar incompetent for forgetting the name of the president of Mexico. When he leveled an attack on her Senate voting record as insufficiently progressive, she glared at him and shot back a line that encapsulates how she—and others in the field—feels about the thirty-eight-year-old former mayor: "I wish everyone was as perfect as you, Pete." She continued, "That's right, I said I made an error. I think having a president that maybe is humble and is able to admit that here and there maybe wouldn't be a bad thing."[9]

But Buttigieg didn't let it go there. He said, "I wouldn't liken this to trivia." He added, "You're staking your candidacy on your Washington experience. You're on the committee that oversees border security. You're on the committee that does trade. You're literally in the part of the committee that's overseeing these things."[10] Surprisingly, Klobuchar seemed to get angry, and although her smile never dimmed, her words were sharp: "Are you trying to say that I'm dumb—are you mocking me here, Pete?" Klobuchar said. "I said I made an error. People sometimes forget names. I am the one that has, No. 1, has the experience based on passing over one hundred bills."[11]

She then criticized Buttigieg's previous failed runs for office. Elizabeth Warren stepped in to defend her friend: "Can I just defend Senator Klobuchar for a minute?" she said. "This is not right. I understand that she forgot a name. It happens, it happens to everybody on this stage. Look, you want to ask about whether or not you understand trade policy with Mexico? Have at it."[12] As author Rebecca Traister wrote in *Good and Mad*, her book about the power of female anger, "Women are not often lauded for their fury,"[13] Klobuchar was also criticized for showing her dislike for Buttigieg—which *Forbes* writer Terina Allen noted was clearly mutual. But Klobuchar would likely get fallout from that too, Allen wrote, "Given that Klobuchar is a woman, she'll likely be the one to suffer any blow back because she directly and openly demonstrated it."[14] RealClearPolitics summed up the Klobuchar-Buttigieg exchange with the headline "Minnesota Nice Gets Nasty: Klobuchar Snaps at Buttigeig."[15]

A Midwestern Pragmatist with Ivy League Credentials

Amy Klobuchar was born in Plymouth, Minnesota, to Rose and Jim Klobuchar. She has one younger sister, Beth. Her parents divorced when

Klobuchar was fifteen years old and in high school. The divorce took a serious toll on the family. Amy's relationship with her father, a recovering alcoholic, was not fully restored until he quit drinking in the 1990s.

Klobuchar attended public schools in Plymouth and was the valedictorian at her high school. She received her BA degree magna cum laude in political science in 1982 from Yale University. While at Yale she served as an intern for Walter Mondale, former Minnesota senator and presidential candidate. *Uncovering the Dome*, Klobuchar's book about the ten years of political battles that led to the construction of the Hubert H. Humphrey Metrodome in Minneapolis, grew out of her senior thesis there. After she graduated from Yale, she enrolled at the University of Chicago Law School, where she served as an associate editor of the University of Chicago Law Review and earned her law degree in 1985. After graduating from law school, Klobuchar returned to Minnesota to work as a corporate lawyer. The birth of her daughter, who was born with a condition that required her to remain in the hospital, plunged her into political activism. She lobbied for legislation that would guarantee new mothers a forty-eight-hour hospital stay, a proposal that eventually became federal law. She was elected prosecutor for the state's most populous county in 1998 and became the first elected female senator from her state in 2006. First elected as a Democrat to the Senate in 2006, she was reelected in 2012 and again in 2018. She serves on the Senate Judiciary Committee, Commerce, Science and Transportation Committee; the Agriculture, Nutrition and Forestry Committee; and the Joint Economic Committee. She also serves as ranking member of the Rules and Administration Committee. In the Democratic Party, she serves as chair of the U.S. Senate Democratic Steering and Outreach Committee.

In the Senate she has focused on issues like immigration, curbing the cost of prescription drugs, addressing sexual harassment, and protecting online privacy. A 2019 Vanderbilt University study found that she was among the most legislatively successful members of the Senate.

She announced her presidential race during a blizzard-like February snowstorm and paid tribute to her parents in her presidential announcement speech:

My dad, whose here with us today at age ninety, got a two-year degree from Vermilion Junior College, and then finished up at the University of Minnesota. He became a journalist. As a young Associated Press reporter, he called the 1960 presidential race for John F. Kennedy. He covered the 1968 conventions. He interviewed everyone from Mike Ditka to Hubert Humphrey to Ronald Reagan to Ginger Rogers. Freedom of the press wasn't some abstract idea to dad. He embraced it. He lived it.

My mom, a proud union member, taught second grade in the suburbs until she was seventy years old. Her students, now grown, still come up to me on the street and tell me she was their favorite teacher.[16]

She underscored her middle-class roots:

"I don't come from money," Klobuchar said as snow began accumulating on her head. "But what I do have is this: I have grit. I have family. I have friends. I have neighbors. I have all of you who are willing to come out in the middle of the winter, all of you who took the time to watch us today from home, all of you who are willing to stand up and say people matter."[17]

One of her sharpest moments came during the fifth Democratic debate, hosted by MSNBC and *The Washington Post* in Atlanta, when she declared, women are held to a higher standard.

First of all, I made very clear I think Pete [Buttigeig] is qualified to be up on this stage, and I am honored to be standing next to him. But what I said is true. Women are held to a higher standard. Otherwise we could play a game called "Name Your Favorite Woman President," which we can't do because it has all been men, including all vice presidents being men. And I think any working woman out there, any woman that's at home, knows exactly what I mean. We have to work harder, and that's a fact. But I want to dispel one thing, because for so long, why has this been happening? I don't think you have to be the tallest person on this stage to be president. I don't think you have to be the skinniest person. I don't think you have to have the loudest voice on this stage. I don't think that means you will be the one that should be president. I think what matters is if you're smart, if you're competent and if you get things done. I am the one that has passed over one hundred bills as the lead Democrat in that gridlock of Washington in Congress on this stage. I think you've got to win, and I am the one, Mr. Vice President, that has been able to win every red and purple congressional district as a lead on a ticket every time. I govern both with my head and my heart. And if you think a woman can't beat Donald Trump, Nancy Pelosi does it every single day.[18]

Klobuchar's profile as an articulate, commonsense, plainspoken, and yet deeply experienced contender grew with each debate. Her persona as "The Senator Next Door"[19] (the title of her autobiography) seemed to recede as she moved more and more into the national spotlight. Senator Klobuchar grew from a bespectacled introvert earlier in her career to a smooth, smiling national figure who, as a skilled debater, distinguished herself among the contenders. She stood out in the debate right after the Iowa caucuses, where she came in fifth, behind former vice president Biden. An app malfunction delayed the final results of the caucus, making it difficult to tell if any candidate really got helped or hurt by the event. But when the final count came through, Klobuchar's final numbers were not far from those of the former vice president, who had been leading in national polls and seemed to be the likely nominee, despite his poor performances and lagging polls.

She went after Buttigieg by assailing his lack of experience and Sanders by charging that his health care plan was "not real," since two-thirds of Democrats in the Senate were not on board with it. She was clear, forceful, and direct in this debate, especially at the end when she articulated a clear case against Trump.

Using both humor and seriousness, she responded effectively to Buttigieg's argument that it was time to move away from the politics of the past to meet the moment that is in front of them. She quipped, "I am listening to this about meeting the moment, and my first thought is, I'm a fresh face up here for a presidential debate. And I figure, Pete, that fifty-nine—my age—is the new thirty-eight up here." The audience laughed, but then she continued, more seriously: "The second thing I think about is this: And that is meeting the moment. We *had* a moment the last few weeks, Mayor, and that moment was these impeachment hearings. And there was a lot of courage that you saw from only a few people. There was courage from Doug Jones, our friend from Alabama, who took that tough vote. There was courage from Mitt Romney, who took a very, very difficult vote. There was courage, as I read today, about Lt. Col. [Alexander] Vindman being escorted out of the White House. What he did took courage."[20]

She then turned Buttigieg's glib words against him: "But what you said, Pete, as you were campaigning through Iowa, as three of us were jurors in that impeachment hearing—you said it was exhausting to watch and that you wanted to turn the channel and watch cartoons." She then added:

> It is easy to go after Washington because that's a popular thing to do. It is much harder—as I see [New Hampshire] Senator [Jeanne] Shaheen, in the front row, such a leader—it is much harder to lead, and much harder to take those difficult positions. Because I think this going after every single thing that people do, because it's popular to say and makes you look like a cool newcomer—I just, I don't think that's what people want right now.

And then, her zinger: "We have a newcomer in the White House and look where it got us. I think having some experience is a good thing."[21] That style of stacking her argument is a debate skill that Klobuchar performs well, and she brings her point to a crescendo when she does it. Pete Buttigieg's face seemed to redden a bit deeper with each of her points.

A few days after her uplifting third-place finish in the New Hampshire primary, Klobuchar appeared on a CNN Town Hall event with CNN host Anderson Cooper. As her poll numbers increased, she faced deeper scrutiny, especially about her standing with the African American community. Klobuchar, who before running for Senate worked as county attorney for Minnesota's largest county, defended her criminal justice record at the town hall, telling voters in Nevada that "anyone that's worked in the criminal justice system knows there's institutional racism."[22]

Klobuchar tried to defend her record by saying, "And when I was there, I worked hard on, for instance, doing more when it came to white-collar crime, doing more with drug courts. And while there were still disparities in our system, like there were any, we had still managed in the eight years to reduce the African American incarceration rate by 12 percent."[23] Her support among African Americans was low, as her record as hard-hitting prosecutor for Hennepin County would become an issue for her.

As the race approached Super Tuesday on March 3, Joe Biden's candidacy was picking up speed. He had exceeded all expectations in the South Carolina primary and had a runaway victory. It looked like it would probably come down to a two-man primary race between Bernie Sanders and Joe Biden. Many moderate Democrats were expressing concern over a possible Bernie Sanders nomination, because for many Democrats Bernie Sanders's politics seemed too far left. The support for moderate Democratic politics was likely the motivation for two rising Democratic moderate stars—Pete Buttigieg and Amy Klobuchar—to bow out of the race just ahead of Super Tuesday and endorse Joe Biden's candidacy. In her endorsement of Joe Biden, Amy Klobuchar said:

> "It is up to us, all of us, to put our country back together, to heal this country and then to build something even greater," she said at a big Biden campaign event in Dallas, Texas a day before Super Tuesday. "I believe we can do this together, and that is why today I am ending my campaign and endorsing Joe Biden for president."

As reported by *The New York Times*, Klobuchar said Biden "can bring our country together and build that coalition of our fired-up Democratic base, and it is fired up, as well as Independents and moderate Republicans, because we do not in our party want to just eek [*sic*] by a victory. We want to win big. And Joe Biden can do that."[24] She told a story about Franklin Delano Roosevelt's connection with working-class Americans, comparing Biden favorably to FDR. "Joe knows you, and he will fight for you."[25] Also endorsing Joe Biden prior to Super Tuesday was Beto O'Rourke, then a congressman from Texas, Pete Buttigieg, and Kamala Harris. Biden was rapidly picking up the support he would need to be the Democratic nominee. Klobuchar was frequently described as a potential running mate for Biden, although after protest and destruction erupted over the death of George Floyd in Minneapolis, her seven-year record as prosecutor there faced renewed scrutiny as she prepared to be vetted as a leading vice presidential contender. In Minneapolis, the police force had long faced accusations of racism and complaints of abuse. But "Klobuchar declined to bring charges against multiple police officers who were involved in shootings during her seven-year tenure," *The New York Times* reported. "Instead she often opted to send cases to a grand jury, a common practice at the time but one that some law enforcement experts say favors police officers."[26]

AMY KLOBUCHAR WAS CAST AS MEAN IN THE PRESS

What happened to the slogan "Minnesota Nice" when it comes to the media framing of Amy Klobuchar's campaign for president? The most significant press she received as she launched her presidential bid and was beginning to be known by the American public came in a series of articles that accused her of being a horrible, mean boss. (Reportedly, Klobuchar demeaned staff in emails and once threw a binder that accidentally hit an aide.) She responded to the criticism, but it seemed to stick. Almost a year after she became a candidate, she was still answering questions from voters who questioned her treatment of staff. In New Hampshire, she responded as follows to a voter concerned about this issue. "First of all, I love my staff, and one of the reasons we're so successful, it's not me, it's them. And I am tough on people, and you can always be better. And I push some people, and as a result, a few of them didn't like me." She also pointed out that nearly seventy current and former staff members even signed a letter, stating that they had a positive experience working for her.[27]

This likability problem is one that faces female politicians but does not seem to impact male politicians as much. Research results suggest the media has particular influence on judgments of women politicians' likability (the "competent but cold" effect), providing evidence that women politicians need to be vigilant in monitoring their media depictions.[28] In fairness, *The New York Times* ran a story highlighting Klobuchar's sense of humor as well, describing her humorous style as a "clean, 'aw, shucks' approach that conveys her own background as a Midwesterner, a mom and a slightly exasperated politician."[29] She repeatedly told the funny and true story about raising money for her first Senate race by asking her former boyfriends for contributions. "I raised $17,000 from ex-boyfriends," she said. "That is not an expanding base."[30] In his book, *Debatable Humor*, Patrick A. Stewart contends that "having a sense of humor will affect reception of candidates, regardless of whether they are front-runner or second-tier candidates. Specifically, notes Stewart, an assistant professor of political science at the University of Arkansas, "by inducing a sense of social solidarity through the emotional contagion of laughter, candidates will likely garner more media attention."[31]

Being characterized as a mean boss seemed especially gendered, and we know that women displaying anger is more sharply criticized than men who do the same thing. Women in particular have been conditioned to suppress their emotions. When women speak out they are often described as shrill, strident, or hysterical. These descriptions of women often raise questions about women candidates and misogyny. As *The Atlantic* pointed out, *"If a man threw a binder at his employees, he'd be appointed president for life*, is the thinking. *An American city would be renamed for him; women would compete to bear him sons; his picture would be printed on currency.* Certainly a kind of sexism has accompanied the incident, and the proof is that Klobuchar seems to be surviving these reports, while a man never would."[32]

Klobuchar addressed a question about how she would "change the rules" when it comes to how misogyny and sexism rear its head, not only for candidates but for women in general. She said that while a lot of attention goes to "rich and famous people" accused of sexual harassment, she believes it is important to fight for people who suffer sexual harassment or inappropriate behavior in everyday work environments—the hotel worker, the factory worker, the nurse. Klobuchar underscored her commitment to safe workplaces for all by saying that she introduced a bill in the Senate with a Republican coauthor that changed the sexual harassment reporting process for the entire U.S. Congress: "It says, one, we are not going to hide this any more, we're going to have a clear process for people who bring cases, and, two, if a member violates the laws and harasses someone they will have to pay for it, and not the taxpayers."[33]

And yet, despite her almost constant smile, her quick wit, and her solid policies, flashes of her anger did emerge, such as during the debate when Pete Buttigieg criticized her for not being able to name the Mexican president. "Her problem is rage, easily uncorked, and directed not at the various forces that might thwart the needs of her constituents, but at the people—many of them young—who work for her."[34] *The New York Times* reported that she "feared sabotage from her own team."[35] Her response was always, "Am I a tough boss sometimes? Yes. Have I pushed people too hard? Yes."[36]

In her first Senate race, Klobuchar was outspent by her opponent two to one, and still managed to eke out a victory. But in presidential politics, the ability to raise money is crucial for success. In 2019, Klobuchar raised $4.8 million between July and the end of September, a total that topped her haul from the previous quarter by $1 million. Her third-quarter fundraising was a fraction of the amount raised by top Democratic candidates such as Bernie Sanders, who raised the most of any candidate in the field, $25.3 million. But it is likely enough to keep Klobuchar's campaign functioning as she attempts to secure more support.[37] She also got a tremendous fundraising boost after the debate right before the New Hampshire primary, and another boost when she finished third in New Hampshire, pulling in 2.5 million.

Klobuchar appealed to many primary voters who did not feel comfortable with the far-left politics of Bernie Sanders and Elizabeth Warren. Klobuchar's main argument—that she can win—resonated with enough voters to sustain Klobuchar's campaign right up until she endorsed Joe Biden. She became a more confident and comfortable national campaigner as the election progressed and she stayed on her message, delivering some of the most memorable lines in debates. Her messages, delivered in a folksy, yet knowledgeable way, clearly described why Republican policies would be tragic for the middle class—such as raising the cost of prescription drugs, making health care harder for people to get, and continuing to ravage the climate. Her plan for what America needs includes taking steps to ensure that take-home pay for middle-class Americans is higher and raising taxes on rich Americans who can afford to pay more.

AMY KLOBUCHAR'S PUBLIC SPEAKING

Amy Klobuchar's common sense and intelligence come through in her public speaking. While conservative syndicated columnist Jonah Goldberg described her as "boringly competent,"[38] Klobuchar seemed to grow more compelling and less ordinary as her presidential bid progressed. There may even have been a longing among the American people for some degree of ordinariness, steadiness, or even "boringness," after the unpredictable public speaking style of Donald Trump, who described being presidential as "boring."[39] Klobuchar is an experienced politician with a strong track record of electability and legislative success. It is of her experience, interwoven with her Midwestern upbringing, that she spoke. She often described her childhood; in debates and speeches also provided evidence of the work that she had done in the Senate to show that she is not just a talker but a doer. She would call attention to herself to say that she is not going to be flashy as a candidate, and that she will probably not have a "viral moment."

Disposition

October 16 on MSNBC Morning Joe she talks about winning with "not exactly a celebrity candidate, but one that fits. And that's me."[40]

An acknowledgment of her low-key style, and an example of Klobuchar's pragmatic approach to policies and her rhetoric, can be found in the declarative statement she made to potential supporters in Waterloo, Iowa, as she considered the potential impact of the second presidential debate: "I'm not going to have this huge viral moment. I hope I do, but I'm not going to do something crazy just to have it."[41]

Klobuchar is the embodiment of "Minnesota nice"—polite and intent on being able to "disagree without being disagreeable," as she wrote in her 2015 memoir, *The Senator Next Door.* In an era of Twitter rants and senatorial showboats, she is the worker bee in the background, tallying up how many of her bills get signed into law: twenty-four, she said, since Trump became president.

Klobuchar told deeply personal and yet highly relatable middle-class stories, including cautionary, clear explanations of how four more years of Republican policies would devastate the middle class. She clearly argued how Republican policies would make prescription drugs more expensive, health insurance harder to get, and climate destruction worse. Her own life is a testament to what a smart, driven person can do to rise to political fame even though her family background provided her with no political advantages.

Style

Amy Klobuchar's typical use of language in her speeches—her rhetorical style—has several characteristics, including her use of humor, agile mind, and quick retorts, and her penchant to remind audiences that she is a Midwesterners with middle-class values and moderate political views who cannot magically wave a wand to change the country. She teaches through her speeches, by explaining that it is easy to promise many things when you are a candidate but delivering is something she can do because she has done it as senator. A practical, albeit unsexy approach to presidential politics is the style of Klobuchar. Her motive for entering politics, having been rushed out of the hospital after the delivery of her only child, her daughter Abigail, is a frame she uses to argue for health care laws and the improvement of medical care for women.

Delivery

Amy Klobuchar is a comfortable and reliably strong public speaker. She seems to enjoy public speaking, smiling throughout her speeches. Her short dark brown hair was always styled fashionably, and she wore skirt suits and pantsuits in solid colors. Amy Klobuchar has the ability to inject humor into her talks, relying on her sharp wit to add flair to what is more often a plainspoken and able to break down complicated policy issues for average Americans to understand easily. For example, in her presidential announcement speech she tried to explain the importance of reigning in "big tech."

She asked:

What would I do as President?

We need to put some digital rules of the road into law when it comes to privacy.

For too long the big tech companies have been telling you "Don't worry! We've got your back!" while your identities are being stolen and your data is mined.

Our laws need to be as sophisticated as the people who are breaking them. We must revamp our nation's cybersecurity and guarantee net neutrality.

And we need to end the digital divide by pledging to connect every household to the internet by 2022, and that means you rural America. Hey, if they can do it in Iceland, we can do it here.[42]

Her last line, about Iceland, is a typical, slightly funny aside that underscores her wit and her resolve to change the technical laws in the country. Amy Klobuchar is a substantive, serious, yet at times funny speaker with a strong grasp of issues and complete control of the public speaking environment.

Memoria

When Klobuchar delivered her presidential announcement in a fierce Minnesota snowstorm, she communicated her grit by visually showing that nothing can stop her. A polished and confident public speaker, she often speaks succinctly without notes or a prepared speech, but also uses notes and occasionally a teleprompter to deliver longer, more detailed speeches. During her campaign, even when the weather could have been more cooperative, she often brought a self-reliant, "up-by-the-bootstraps" attitude to the delivery of her speeches. Klobuchar frequently smiles throughout her presentations, even when she is saying something that is not necessarily funny or worthy of a smile. For example, when she spoke in Iowa, she continued to smile as she told the stories of farmers who struggled to keep their farms alive. She said:

So when I talk to the workers in places, like the carpenters in western Pennsylvania or dairy farmers in Wisconsin, or dockworkers in Michigan, they told me this—so they hear when people say [President Trump] is a bully, they'll acknowledge this.

But then they say, "You know what really bugs me? What really bugs me is that I have to work so hard just to be able to make sure my family can have a mortgage or just to be able to afford insulin, or just to be able to afford to send my kid to school."

"And when things go bad for me," they say, "I just have to work harder. When the dairy farming, which has been a big struggle, and things go bad, I've got to take out an extra loan or I've gotta be able to, or my spouse goes and takes an extra job." And then they look at him, and they think to themselves, "You know, he's got the best job in the world. He lives in the nicest house."[43]

OBSTACLES TO HER PRESIDENTIAL BID

Amy Klobuchar purposely argued that she was not the most exciting person in the race, but that she could deliver a win and that her record showed legislative success. By the time she stepped out of the race to endorse Joe Biden for president, she had become nationally known and respected for her intelligence and pragmatic approach to politics. But could she excite the electorate? As mentioned, Klobuchar seemed to get better and better as her campaign for president continued; thus, there was reason to believe that she could have excited the electorate, especially if voters considered her winning record in Minnesota. Like Hillary Clinton, who voters may have thought less than exciting or lacking charisma, Klobuchar almost seemed like the antipolitician—or at least, as Clinton put it, "not a natural politician." To be a changemaker, like Bill Clinton or Barack Obama (two natural politicians), a requisite amount of charisma is needed. Klobuchar seemed to get close to charismatic, but not quite there.

The early media reports about how mean a boss she could be seemed to stick with some voters. No matter how funny she was on late-night television or how winning she was in Minnesota, the idea that she could be so angry that she would throw things would be more disqualifying for a woman that for a man.

After Her Presidential Bid

In April 2020, after she had dropped out of the race, Amy Klobuchar penned an opinion piece in *The New York Times* about the merits of mail-in voting. She wrote:

In Milwaukee, which has the largest minority population in the state, the number of open polling places was shrunk to five from 180, as poll workers dropped out.

In Green Bay, the number plunged to two from 31. Needless to say, the lines were hours long. Voters wore homemade face masks to protect themselves from contracting the coronavirus—if they were willing to risk voting at all.

And if you think there ought to be a better way, you're not alone. I know of one person who, with an election approaching in his newly adopted state, simply requested an absentee ballot from the comfort of his own home—so he could vote safely and easily by mail.[44]

Running for president put Amy Klobuchar on the radar for many Americans who had not previously heard of her, even after her distinguishing rhetorical turn at the Brett Kavanaugh hearings. But pieces like the *New York Times* op-ed gave her opportunities to display her grasp of important issues and her direct, persuasive way of explaining them:

In a democracy, no one should be forced to choose between health and the right to vote.

Imagine if days before the November election you learn that your polling place has been closed, that your request for an absentee ballot has gone unfulfilled and that you have to risk a grave infection by standing in line—possibly for hours—to claim your stake in our democracy.

If that sounds outrageous to you, it should. But it's exactly what happened in the Wisconsin election last week.[45]

After her husband John was struck with Covid-19, Klobuchar spoke about the deadly nature of the disease. Sharing that no one knew how he had contracted it, she confronted a fundamental truth about the pandemic and the strength of the virus causing it. "If you have someone that healthy get that sick," she realized, "it can happen to anyone."[46]

As the country awaited Joe Biden's selection of a running mate in late June 2020, Klobuchar took herself out of the running in the midst of social unrest over the death of George Floyd and the entire "Black Lives Matter" movement. She said, "This is a historic moment, and America must seize on this moment. And I truly believe, as I actually told the vice president last night when I called him, that I think this is a moment to put a woman of color on that ticket."[47]

Speaking on the opening night of the Democratic National Convention, Klobuchar began her talk with one of the most important topics of the election: the viability of the U.S. Postal Service. "Hello America!" she said, smiling broadly. "I believe that the right to vote is fundamental, and the post office is essential." Still smiling, Klobuchar then delivered one of the zingy one-liners she's well-known for: "The President may hate the post office, but he is still going to have to send them a 'change of address' card come January."[48] She then became serious about what is at stake in the 2020 election. She reminded the audience that she had run for president, but gladly stepped down to endorse Joe Biden's candidacy—all in the same day, describing Biden as a man of "scrappy, working-class roots."[49]

By running for president, Amy Klobuchar has become a national figure. She is still "the senator next door,"[50] but she is also a viable presidential candidate in the future. Like Harris she has shown that speaking up can place you in a leadership position for the future. Both Kamala Harris and Amy Klobuchar became nationally recognized when they questioned Brett Kavanaugh pointedly during his Supreme Court nomination hearing. They built upon the national recognition they acquired to make a presidential bid. Amy Klobuchar is now well-known and may likely reemerge on the national political stage.

NOTES

1. WMUR, Transcript of Amy Klobuchar's New Hampshire Primary Speech, February 12, 2020, https://www.wmur.com/article/amy-klobuchar-new-hampshire-primary-night-speech/30884135# (accessed February 17, 2020).

2. Ibid.

3. Ibid.

4. Ibid.

5. Ibid.

6. Ibid.

7. Liz Entman, "Grassley, Klobuchar Most Effective Senators of 115th Congress According to Study," Vanderbilt University, February 28, 2019, https://news.vanderbilt.edu/2019/02/28/grassley-klobuchar-most-effective-senators-of-115th-congress-according-to-study/ (accessed February 12, 2020).

8. "Buttigieg and Klobuchar Go Round and Round in Las Vegas," https://www.youtube.com/watch?v=A9_J9M3HJo4 (accessed May 11, 2020).

9. Ibid.

10. Ibid.

11. Ibid.

12. https://www.nytimes.com/2020/02/20/us/politics/democratic-debate-las-vegas.html?action=click&module=Top%20Stories&pgtype=Homepage.

13. Rebecca Traister, *Good and Mad: The Revolutionary Power of Women's Anger* (New York: Simon and Schuster, 2018), 4.

14. Terina Allen, "'Are You Mocking Me?' Amy Klobuchar Isn't Just Fighting For The Nomination—She's Fighting For Her Career," *Forbes*, February 20, 2020, https://www.forbes.com/sites/terinaallen/2020/02/20/are-you-mocking-me-why-it-boiled-over-between-amy-klobuchar-and-pete-buttigieg/#2b04703e4b94 (accessed September 10, 2020).

15. Phillip Wegmann, "Minnesota Nice Gets Nasty," RealClear Politics, February 20, 2020, https://www.realclearpolitics.com/articles/2020/02/20/minnesota_nice_gets_nasty_klobuchar_snaps_at_buttigieg__142446.html (accessed September 11, 2020).

16. Ibid.

17. Alan Epstein, "Amy Klobuchar fans braved a blizzard to watch her 2020 US presidential bid announcement," *Quartz*, February 10, 2019 https://qz.com/1547041/amy-klobuchar-fans-braved-a-blizzard-to-watch-her-2020-us-presidential-bid-announcement/ (accessed October 11, 2019).

18. Kate Sullivan, "Klobuchar: If you think a woman can't beat Trump, 'Nancy Pelosi does it every single day'" CNN, November 20, 2019 https://www.cnn.com/2019/11/20/politics/amy-klobuchar-woman-trump-nancy-pelosi-debate/index.html (accessed May 11, 2020).

19. Amy Klobuchar, *The Senator Next Door* (New York: Henry Holt, 2015).

20. Ibid.

21. Maggie Astor, "Amy Klobuchar Compares Pete Buttigieg to Trump," *The New York Times*, February 8, 2020 (accessed February 8, 2020).

22. Ryan Beene, Bill Allison, and Hailey Wallter, "Klobuchar's Rise Brings New Scrutiny to Record as Prosecutor, February 16, 2020, https://www.bloomberg.com/news/articles/2020-02-16/klobuchar-says-she-s-raised-12-million-online-since-n-h-debate (accessed February 19, 2020).

23. Ibid.

24. https://www.cnn.com/2020/03/02/politics/amy-klobuchar-ends-2020-campaign/index.html.

25. Ibid.

26. Nick Corasanti and Katie Glueck, "Protests in Minnesota Renew Scrutiny of Klobuchar's Record as Prosecutor," *The New York Times*, May 28, 2020, https://www.nytimes.com/2020/05/29/us/politics/klobuchar-minneapolis-george-floyd.html (accessed May 28, 2020).

27. John Verhovek, "Senator Amy Klobuchar Talks Immigration and Healthcare," ABC News, ttps://abcnews.go.com/Politics/table-sen-amy-klobuchar-talks-immigration-health-care/story?id=66692110 (accessed February 12, 2020).

28. K.L. Winfrey and J.M. Schnoebelen, (2019). Running as a Woman (or Man): A Review of Research on Political Communicators and Gender Stereotypes, *Review of Communication Research*, 7, 109-138, doi: 10.12840/ISSN.2255- 4165.020.

29. Jennifer Medina, "A Little Bit Stand-Up, and a Little Bit Stump Speech," *The New York Times*, November 7, 2019. A10.

30. Ibid.

31. Patrick A Stewart, *Debatable Humor: Laughing Matters on the 2008 Presidential Primary Campaign* (Lexington Books, Lanham, MD: 2012).

32. Kate Flanagan, "The Anger of Amy Klobuchar," *The Atlantic*, March 5, 2019. https://www.theatlantic.com/ideas/archive/2019/03/telling-reactions-tales-amy-klobuchars-rage/584104/ (accessed May 27, 2020).

33. CNN Town Hall, February 27, 2020, https://www.cnn.com/videos/politics/2020/02/27/amy-klobuchar-sexism-effective-leadership-south-carolina-town-hall-vpx.cnn (accessed February 28, 2020).

34. Flanagan, "The Anger of Amy Klobuchar."

35. Matt Flegenheimer and Sydney Ember, "How Amy Klobuchar Treats Her Staff," *The New York Times*, February 22, 2019, A-1.

36. Ibid.

37. Dan Mercia, Kyung Lah, Jasmine Wright and Kate Sullivan, "Amy Klobuchar ends 2020 campaign and endorses Joe Biden," CNN Politics, https://www.cnn .com/2020/03/02/politics/amy-klobuchar-ends-2020-campaign/index.html, (accessed March 3, 2020) https://www.politico.com/news/2019/10/07/klobuchar-48-million -third-quarter-0382281.

38. Jonah Goldberg, "Biden Facing a Marketing Decision on His Running Mate," *The Morning Call* (Allentown, PA) May 28, 2020, 17.

39. Peter Baker, "On Day 1,001, Trump Made It Clear: Being 'Presidential' Is Boring," *The New York Times*, October 18, 2019. https://www.nytimes.com/2019/10 /18/us/politics/trump-presidency.html (accessed May 28, 2020).

40. MSNBC Morning Joe, October 16, 2019. https://www.msnbc.com/morn-ing-joe/watch/amy-klobuchar-says-she-s-not-a-celebrity-candidate-71367749735 (accessed October 17, 2019).

41. Reid J. Epstein, "Candidates Are Pushed to Go Viral, or Risk Being Left Behind," *The New York Times*, July 20, 2019, A20.

42. Amy Klobuchar, presidential announcement remarks, *Twin Cities Pioneer Press*, February 9, 2019 https://www.twincities.com/2019/02/10/amy-klobuchars-big -speech-today-heres-a-sneak-peak/ (accessed January 6, 2021).

43. Lisa Lerer, "Amy Klobuchar: The senator from Minnesota wants to lower drug prices and bridge the rural-urban divide," *The New York Times*, January 31, 2020, "https://www.nytimes.com/interactive/2020/01/31/us/politics/amy-klobuchar -campaign-speech.html," (accessed September 2, 2020).

44. Amy Klobuchar, "Amy Klobuchar: The Right Way to Vote This November," *The New York Times*, April 14, 2020, https://www.nytimes.com/2020/04/14/opinion/ klobuchar-coronavirus-mail-voting.html (accessed May 27, 2020).

45. Amy Klobuchar, "Amy Klobuchar: The Right Way to Vote This November," *The New York Times*, April 14, 2020. https://www.nytimes.com/2020/04/14/opinion/ klobuchar-coronavirus-mail-voting.html (accessed April 15, 2020).

46. Jim Spencer, "Minnesota Sen. Amy Klobuchar details husband's ordeal with COVID-19," *Star Tribune*, March 29, 2020. https://www.startribune.com/minnesota -sen-amy-klobuchar-s-ordeal-with-husband-s-covid-19/569190792/.

47. Jasmine Wright, "Amy Klobuchar Drops out of Biden VP contention and says he should choose a woman of color," CNN, June 19, 2020, cnn.com/klobuchardrop-sout/19June2020 (accessed June 20, 2020).

48. Amy Klobuchar, "Sen. Amy Klobuchar's full speech at the Democratic National Convention," PBS Newshour, August 17, 2020. https://www.youtube.com/ watch?v=HdpJghiklGA (accessed August 18, 2020).

49. Ibid.

50. Klobuchar, *The Senator Next Door*.

Chapter 5

Elizabeth Warren

A Professor Turns a Country into Her Classroom

We can all remember a moment when we wanted to share something—in a classroom, at a dinner table, or maybe in a boardroom—but instead of being given the platform, we were silenced. A scenario that is repeated again and again in the history of women and leadership in the United States, it happened in 2017 to U.S. senator Elizabeth Warren when she spoke against confirming Senator Jeff Sessions of Alabama as U.S. attorney general. Senator Warren quoted a 1986 statement from the late senator Ted Kennedy regarding Sessions's nomination to federal court judge, describing Sessions as a "disgrace to the Justice Department."[1] She then began to read from a letter that Coretta Scott King had written at that time to the Senate Judiciary Committee. In a ten-page statement accompanying her letter, King had argued that Sessions "has used the awesome power of his office to chill the free exercise of the vote by black citizens in the district he now seeks to serve as a federal judge."

Following a Senate ruling to silence Senator Warren, Senator Mitch McConnell said on the Senate floor, "Senator Warren was giving a lengthy speech. She had appeared to violate the rule. She was warned. She was given an explanation. Nevertheless, she persisted." The phrase "Nevertheless, she persisted" became a feminist slogan and made Warren an instant feminist icon. Immortalized on T-shirts, books, bumper stickers, the phrase functioned as a reminder that to be a successful woman, one must keep going, no matter what. The concept that she would not be silenced would become an ideal one to counter the bombastic rhetoric of Donald Trump, and one that would be instantly identified by other women who have ever been talked over by a boss, husband, or any other male figure.

When Elizabeth Warren announced her presidential 2020 campaign on a cold morning in Lawrence, Massachusetts, in January 2019, she began with an instructive story, much like the one she offered on the floor of the Senate, and one that a professor might begin with to explain economic policies to a class.

I want to tell you a story.

A little over 100 years ago, textile mills in Lawrence like the ones behind us today employed tens of thousands of people, and immigrants flocked here from more than 50 countries for a chance to work at the looms.

Lawrence was one of the centers of American industry.

Business was booming. The guys at the top were doing great, but workers made so little money that families were forced to crowd together in dangerous tenements and live on beans and scraps of bread.

Inside the mills, working conditions were horrible.

Children were forced to operate dangerous equipment.

Workers lost hands, arms and legs in the gears of machines.

One out of every three adult mill workers died by the time they were 25.

Then, on January 11, 1912, a group of women who worked right here at the Everett Mill discovered that the bosses had cut their pay.

And that was it—the women said "enough is enough." They shut down their looms and walked out.

Soon workers walked out at another mill in town.

Then another. Then another—until 20,000 textile workers across Lawrence were on strike. These workers—led by women—didn't have much. Not even a common language.

Nevertheless . . . they persisted!

They organized. They embraced common goals. They translated the minutes of their meetings into 25 different languages, so that the English and Irish workers who had been here for years and the Slavic and Syrian workers new to America could stand together.

They hammered out their demands:

- Fair wages
- Overtime pay
- and the right to join a union.[2]

These were the themes that led to Warren's rise to national fame, her Senate bid, and her presidential run: that big businesses keep the average worker from making a good living, and thus, a good life. As her storytelling concluded, the point became clear: by banding together and fighting, the average worker could get ahead. She offered herself as the leader of the fight, and it was a message that would resonate with voters because, like them, they saw Warren also as middle class—one of them.

ELIZABETH WARREN, THE RESEARCHER, THE THINKER, THE BANKRUPTCY LAW PROFESSOR

She brought her considerable intellect and energy to her race for the presidency and seemed to be poised for success as the candidate with the best, most well-conceived plans, the most organized operation, and the most energetic, carefully considered and constructed message to give middle-class Americans a fair shake. Elizabeth Warren had previously been a memorable surrogate for Hillary Clinton, calling Donald Trump "a loser" and "toxic" in 2016. Warren's efforts on Clinton's behalf seemed a good trial run for her own bid for president, and 2020 seemed like her time. A formidable debater and indefatigable campaigner, Warren seemed to have it all figured out. But the word "electable" kept creeping into her interviews with media. While this is a word that male candidates rarely if ever hear, the press and public wondered aloud if she was just that—"electable." According to Maggie Kennedy, a field organizer with the Warren for President campaign, "We would hear everything they liked or didn't like about her. Everybody wants to be a pundit. Everyone wants to have something to say or an explanation for everything, and we heard that word—electable—a lot. My answer to a lot of people is that no one is electable until they are elected, and Elizabeth Warren won every race she entered before she ran for the presidency."[3]

For years, women who have broken down barriers have been left off the history book pages. If they did not seem to check every box, meet every qualification, often they would be excluded as symbolic candidates for office—or any other venture that seemed outside the small sphere of actions that women before them had already taken. Mike Bloomberg, who spent half a billion dollars running ads to become the next Democratic presidential nominee, had hoped to become the moderate voice in a big field of candidates. But despite his massive spending, even he (and his campaign operation) could not see a clear nominee emerging from the large pack of Democratic hopefuls. Among these many hopefuls was former vice president Joseph R. Biden Jr., who seemed unable to articulate his vision and capture the interest of the public and donors, until later in the primary season when a number of Democratic hopefuls offered their endorsements.

Bloomberg, no star orator himself, and at best rusty debater, turned in shaky performances in two debates before he appeared on the ballot for the first time on Super Tuesday. When a reporter asked Bloomberg how he would feel if, on Super Tuesday, he came in third place, Bloomberg responded that "if there's only three candidates, you can't do worse than that." "Well, there is Elizabeth Warren also," the reporter replied. "I didn't realize she's still in," Bloomberg replied. "Is she?"[4] It seems unlikely that Bloomberg could have forgotten Warren, who had eviscerated him on the debate stage, questioning him pointedly about his treatment of women. And yet, for anyone who studies women and presidential politics, the idea that Warren was simply forgotten is, sadly, a familiar one.

Elizabeth Warren's energetic political rallies feature the earnest, thorough, and thoughtful law-professor-turned-politician who routinely dashes on to the stage and introduces herself each time in the same way—by saying, "Hi! I'm Elizabeth Warren and I'm running for President!"

This "maybe you have not heard of me" type of introduction squares perfectly with her constantly striving "schoolmarm" persona—the one who is twice as prepared as anyone else but sure she will fail the test.

Irrespective of how much her true nature may be that of an introverted bookworm, by the time Elizabeth Warren ran for president in 2020, she had become a very warm and engaging storyteller who seemed as natural a politician as there ever was one. She shares her message that stems from her scholarly research on how the economy works against the average American, while it simultaneously rewards millionaires and billionaires.

One of her most often recounted tales is of her own journey as a brainy, only daughter with three older brothers, growing up in a middle-class, blue-collar, Republican Oklahoma family that struggled financially. She included stories of her early life, and her three older brothers into her speeches, including when her oldest brother, Donald Reed, died of Covid-19. She brings her experience as a teacher and an educator to her campaigns. Her intelligence shines through when asked questions, and her years of making challenging material understandable are evident. She is agile not only on the economy but also on foreign policy, specifically on restoring relations with NATO. She is committed to anti-corruption legislation. Of all the Democratic hopefuls, she was arguably the most on message. She was quite disciplined on promoting a narrow set of core priorities—cracking down on Wall Street, helping student borrowers, and giving the middle class more financial opportunities—while stubbornly refusing to get sucked into the political controversies and media mayhem that often plague Democratic campaigns. This distinguished her early in the race and demonstrated her well-thought-out plans and longtime commitment to policymaking. She offered plans to sharply increase the federal investment in clean energy research and to wean the American economy from fossil fuels.

In the final debate before the Iowa caucus, Warren accused Bernie Sanders of saying, a few weeks before the 2020 campaign started, that he didn't think a woman could win the presidency in 2016. Because the remark was allegedly made in a private conversation, we will never know for sure what was said. Sanders, for his part, vociferously denied ever saying it. It came up during the debate in Iowa and Sanders tried to avoid having to address the situation.

But Warren was not nearly as ready to let Sanders off the hook. Her response to Sanders led to the night's most memorable exchange. While

Sanders had insisted that everyone knows a woman can beat Trump, Warren said persistent sexism is undeniable.

> "Bernie is my friend, and I am not here to try to fight with Bernie," she said. "But, look, this question about whether or not a woman can be president has been raised, and it's time for us to attack it head-on. And I think the best way to talk about who can win is by looking at people's winning record. So, can a woman beat Donald Trump? Look at the men on this stage. Collectively, they have lost 10 elections. The only people on this stage who have won every single election that they've been in are the women. [Minnesota Sen.] Amy [Klobuchar] and me."[5]

And yet, despite this emotional and effective plea, Warren finished third in the Iowa caucus, and seemed to be losing steam as she moved toward the New Hampshire primary. Her strongest rhetorical moments were evident in the debates. In a raucous debate held in South Carolina in late February, Warren said, "Bernie and I agree on a lot of things, but I think I would make a better president than Bernie."[6] She also went after billionaire Mike Bloomberg, attacking his record as a businessman and bringing up in particular an allegation that he told a pregnant employee to "kill it"—referring to the woman's unborn child. Bloomberg fiercely denied the allegation, but acknowledged he sometimes made jokes that were not well received.

When she burst onto the stage at her rallies, the feminist anthems "9 to 5" (written and performed by Dolly Parton) or "Respect" (written by Otis Redding, but made legendary by Aretha Franklin) would often blare through the speakers. The lyrics of "9 to 5" served up part of her rallying cry for the middle class:

They let you dream just to watch 'em shatter
You're just a step on the boss-man's ladder
But you got dreams he'll never take away.[7]

Warren's main thesis, that Washington works for the rich, was echoed in a speech she gave at a New York City rally during her campaign. She said:

> For the rich and the powerful in this country. There are first, second, third, and fourth chances to get ahead. But for a lot of Americans, especially for people of color, there is barely one, or for some, no chance at all. We have the power to fix that. We are the wealthiest nation in the history of the world.[8]

Professor Elizabeth Warren took the same lessons she had been teaching for decades and made the country her classroom. In her books, written over a decade before she ran for president, she warned against how today's families are working harder than ever, [yet] many are in worse financial shape than their parents were.[9]

Her teacherly approach was evident on the day she announced her presidential 2020 campaign in January 2019, in Lawrence, Massachusetts, and continued throughout her campaign.

Sometimes her middle-class advocacy took the form of a feminist lesson, suggesting that Warren, a woman, is saying something now about the condition of America, and like her foremothers, she wants to make it right. Warren, the gifted professor-turned-politician, had pulled herself up from a family that didn't think she deserved an education, from an early marriage, and from a life that seemed to include few prospects. Now she was teaching the country that America had gotten out of whack and that she, as president, would fight for the middle class to make it right again.

FROM OKLAHOMA TO HARVARD
TO THE WHITE HOUSE

Elizabeth Ann Warren was born in Oklahoma in 1949. She is a former academic, a law school professor specializing in bankruptcy law, and a progressive politician. Her campaign focused on consumer rights, economic opportunity, and the social safety net; she also works on these issues in the Senate.

A graduate of the University of Houston and Rutgers Law School, Warren has taught law at several universities, including the University of Houston, the University of Texas at Austin, the University of Pennsylvania, and Harvard University. She was one of the most cited professors in the field of commercial law before beginning her political career. She is the author of three books and the coauthor of six, both academic and for a general audience. Warren's initial foray into public policy began in 1995 when she worked to oppose what eventually became a 2005 law restricting bankruptcy access for individuals. Her national profile rose during the 2000s when she took public stances in favor of more stringent banking restrictions following the 2007–2008 financial crisis. She served as chair of the Congressional Oversight Panel of the Troubled Asset Relief Program (TARP, a U.S. economic program designed to ward off the nation's mortgage and financial crisis). She was instrumental in creating the Consumer Financial Protection Bureau, having been appointed by President Obama to serve as the first special adviser. Especially for a woman who had spent her entire career in higher education, Elizabeth Warren demonstrated her sophisticated understanding of the different levers of power in an administration, particularly in the use of regulation in areas such as trade, antitrust, and environmental policy.

When she first arrived in Washington, during the Great Recession of 2008, Senator Warren distinguished herself as a citizen-politician. She showed an admirable desire to shake off the entrapments of many Washington interests in favor of pragmatic problem-solving on behalf of average Americans.

In 2012, she won the U.S. Senate election in Massachusetts, defeating incumbent Republican Scott Brown to become the first female senator from Massachusetts. She was assigned to the Senate Special Committee on Aging; the Committee on Banking, Housing, and Urban Affairs; and the Committee on Health, Education, Labor, and Pensions.

She campaigned for Hillary Clinton in 2016 and gained a reputation for telling off Donald Trump. A sample of her fiery rhetoric follows, from a speech she gave at a New Hampshire rally, just a couple of weeks before Election Day:

> Donald Trump is incapable—physically incapable—of showing an ounce of respect to more than half of the human beings in this country.
>
> He thinks because he has money, that he can call women fat pigs and bimbos.
>
> He thinks because he is a celebrity, he can rate women's bodies from one to ten.
>
> He thinks because he has a mouthful of Tic Tacs that he can force himself on any woman within groping distance.[10]

The major themes that emerge in Elizabeth Warren's speeches throughout her entire political career, including her bid for the presidency, are fighting bigotry, building opportunity, and demanding democracy.

In the second primary debate, Elizabeth Warren was accused of "fairy-tale economics" by John Delaney, a former Maryland congressman who tried to convince the audience that both Elizabeth Warren's and Bernie Sanders's economic ideas were too far left and full of "impossible promises." The exchange showcased Warren's astute debate skills, when she shot back: "I don't understand why anybody goes to all the trouble of running for president of the United States just to talk about what we really can't do and shouldn't fight for."[11]

That same kind of on-point, folksy excoriation came during the February 2020 debate, in an exchange with former New York mayor Michael Bloomberg. Rumors of Bloomberg's mistreatment of women in his employ, especially in the midst of the #MeToo environment, were gaining traction. Warren insisted on knowing whether Bloomberg would be willing to release some of the former female employees at his news media organization from the nondisclosure agreements they had signed. But he declined to do so, calling the agreements "consensual" and trying to minimize the underlying complaints by suggesting that the women merely "didn't like a joke I told."[12] After pressing the former mayor, who looked flustered, she proclaimed, "We are not going to beat Donald Trump with a man who has who knows how many nondisclosure agreements and the drip, drip, drip of stories of women saying they have been harassed and discriminated against."[13]

While Elizabeth Warren's rhetoric was sharp, her policy plans well-conceived and thorough, Super Tuesday proved to be a terrific disappointment. She came away with an abysmal third-place finish in her home state of Massachusetts, indicating that liberal votes were split sharply between her and Sanders. Surprising to many was Joe Biden's first-place win in Massachusetts, resurrecting a lackluster campaign full of poor debate performances and tepid campaigning. This was a hard blow for the Warren campaign, since she had also finished poorly in Iowa, Nevada, New Hampshire, and South Carolina. Super Tuesday revealed that Biden and Sanders would be the contenders for the nomination and that, while Warren was the last viable woman in the race, and had so rapidly gained momentum, the Warren campaign just did not have staying power, and there would not be a woman nominee for president of the United States in 2020.

THE END OF HER PRESIDENTIAL CAMPAIGN

Elizabeth Warren looked clearly sad and shaken when she emerged from her home, with her purple winter jacket on, holding her husband Bruce's hand, her dog trailing along, to announce that she would be suspending her campaign. With a crack in her voice, she said:

> So, I announced this morning that I am suspending my campaign for president. I say this with a deep sense of gratitude for every single person who got in this fight, every single person who tried on a new idea. Every single person who just moved a little in their notion of what a president of the United States should look like.
>
> I will not be running for president in 2020, but I guarantee I will stay in the fight for the hardworking folks across this country who've gotten the short end of the stick over and over. That's been the fight of my life and it will continue to be so.

She asked if anyone had a question, and of course, the throngs of media jumped, with the first one seeming to affect Warren the most. A reporter asked:

"I wonder what your message would be to the women and girls who feel like we're left with two white men to decide between?" With a strain in her voice, she said, "I know one of the hardest parts of this is all those pinky promises and all those little girls who are going to have to wait four more years. That's going to be hard." And indeed, Maggie Kennedy, a young field organizer for Warren for President, was especially moved by the pinky promise, saying, "My heart was so warmed when I'd see a little girl's eyes light up as she pinky swore Elizabeth, and when I'd catch the love in her parents' eyes as they looked on with pride."[14]

She did not want to endorse Joe Biden or Bernie Sanders at that moment, noting that she wanted to focus on her suspension of her campaign and what that would mean for her staff and volunteers. She expressed gratitude and concern for her team and said she wanted to give the idea of her endorsement some more thought.

She waited several weeks and mid-April she came out in support of Joe Biden when he appeared to be the presumptive nominee, noting that he "grew up on the ragged edge of the middle class in Scranton, Pennsylvania, and that he knows that a government run with integrity, empathy and heart saves lives."[15]

Like a professor who did not make tenure, or who has published a research paper with a faulty hypothesis, Warren reflected on her reasoning for getting into the race. She said, "You know, I was told at the beginning of this whole undertaking that there are two lanes, a progressive lane that Bernie Sanders is the incumbent for, and a moderate lane that Joe Biden is the incumbent for. And there's no room for anyone else in this. I thought that wasn't right. But evidently, I was wrong."[16]

MEDIA FRAMES

Pocahontas

It was hard to image that Elizabeth Warren would be able overcome the ridicule from the president of the United States, Donald Trump, who continuously mocked her by using the crude ethnic slur "Pocahontas" to call attention to her self-identification in the 1980s and 1990s as part Native American. During a televised debate in 2018, he said that if she agreed to take a DNA test he would donate $1 million to her favorite charity. Warren shot back on Twitter by condemning Trump's practice of separating immigrant children from their parents at the border. "While you obsess over my genes, your Admin is conducting DNA tests on little kids because you ripped them from their mamas," she tweeted.[17] If it had just ended there, perhaps it would have simply receded from public consciousness. On her own, however, Elizabeth Warren brought the topic back into the media when she participated in a video that showed her in her hometown of Norman, Oklahoma, pointing out landmarks and talking to people. She took the bait from the president and had a DNA analysis done, but the results showed only that she had distant Native American ancestry. Because the president is wont to mock, he jumped on the story immediately, mocking her again and announcing, "I have more Indian blood than she has!"

But what was truly worse than the mockery from the president and the bad press was the sharp criticism she received from the Cherokee Nation, which roundly rebuked her for confusing the issue of bloodlines with tribal membership. Warren apologized, but the damage seemed to be done. While this was an unfortunate media frame, it did not quell her early campaign momentum.

Nerdy Professor

"What too many voters see," said Paul Begala, a Democratic strategist who worked on President Bill Clinton's 1992 campaign, "is Professor Warren from Harvard Law and not Betsy from Norman, Oklahoma."[18] While she repeatedly referred to herself as a former schoolteacher, most people knew her as the elite law professor whom Barack Obama recruited to help reform big banking.

At the October 2019 primary debate, Elizabeth Warren was the most attacked by other Democratic rivals, a sign that she was seen as leading the race. At this debate, likely because her poll numbers were increasing at the time, she looked like the candidate to beat. Pete Buttigieg, Amy Klobuchar, and Beto O'Rourke all attacked her comprehensive plans, trying instead to present themselves as the most likely to serve the American people better.

But Warren's early strength as a candidate slipped, and she failed to place higher than third in the caucuses and primaries.

"I get asked this question over and over, about, you know, do you think you face sexism in running for president?" Warren told reporters the night she finished fourth in the Nevada caucuses. "And, you know, there are only two answers and they're both bad. The first one is, 'Uh, yeah,' in which case everybody says, 'Oh, whiner.'"

"The second is to say, 'Oh, no,' in which case, at least every other woman looks at you and thinks, 'What planet is she living on?'"[19]

ELIZABETH WARREN'S PUBLIC SPEAKING

Elizabeth Warren's public speaking style is very much like that of a teacher holding forth in front of a class. As if contemplating how to frame a lesson so that her class could best comprehend, she almost always begins her utterances with a drawn-out "Soooooo . . ." In addition to her public speaking, which took on a folksy tone, Warren also spent a considerable amount of campaign time on the phone—reaching out to activists, celebrities, leaders, local Democratic officials, and even a young boy whose dog passed away to offer her sympathies. She would begin every call in much the same way that she began her public speeches, by introducing herself, "Hi, this is Elizabeth Warren."[20]

Invention

Elizabeth Warren alternated her speeches between two main topics: her biography as a scrappy, Midwestern woman who transcended the norms that most women of her time had relegated to follow to make a difference for middle-class Americans that were increasingly squeezed out of a fair shot at a comfortable, successful life. The later she culled from her years as a professor and author of economics articles and books. She applied stories from her own, lived experiences as well as the experiences of hardworking Americans who can't seem to get ahead because the laws in the country are geared for top earners, not middle-class people. She spoke as one of the many middle-class people, but also as a learned scholar who never forgot her roots, and who strove to help others by applying what she had learned through deep scholarship about the financial conditions of Americans.

Disposition

Warren would often do two things in her stump speeches: begin her speeches with an illustrative story and reveal parts of her biography. She tried to tie her life and the stories she told into the overall problems facing middle-class Americans, and to emphasize—no matter how much they tried to pay their bills or build a solid financial future for their families—that the system was rigged against them.

Her main point was that the rich are getting richer and that the hardworking middle class and poor are going downward. She reiterated one question over and over again, connecting her economics professor past with her politician present: "I spent most of my career studying one simple question: Why do American families go broke?"[21]

Style

Elizabeth Warren's use of language in her speeches is didactic, no doubt a style garnered from her first career path as a teacher and professor. She aims to explain to her audience and help them to understand the often complicated issues of politics and economic structures that she knows well. She used her own life as a case study to apply the principles of economic stability to the nation. While Warren aims to instruct, she is careful not to condescend. Her word choice is more teacher than professor, more of a wise elder aunt than know-it-all, although it is hard to conceal her immense intellect, uncommon for politicians who are in the age of television more camera-ready than deeply knowledgeable on policy issues.

Delivery

Elizabeth Warren's public speaking delivery is energetic and educational. She brings her lessons to life by applying her own family's middle-class circumstances to economic policies that she wishes to champion as president. She is a confident, no-nonsense presenter, who usually wears black pants and top, with a brightly colored blazer on top. In the cold weather, she sported a casual "puffer" style jacket. Tall and slim, she shows her enthusiasm for the United States by often running on stage and moving around constantly as she campaigns and speaks. She often urged Americans to fight for their rights, in one speech saying, "Americans are at our best when we see a problem—we tackle it head on—and we fight it to the ground!"[22]

Memoria

Campaign field organizer Maggie Kennedy told me that Warren "had a basic stump speech that she memorized."[23] However, she always spoke from the heart, and added impromptu anecdotal stories specific to the occasion. She did not use a teleprompter or notes. Usually she had a stool on the stage with a bottle of water underneath it, in case she needed a sip, most often during the question-and-answer period.

Elizabeth Warren rarely spoke from a prepared script. She had committed much of her speeches to memory and through repetition had mastered a delivery that was impactful, polished, and prepared yet of the moment and geared directly to the audience in front of her.

OBSTACLES TO HER PRESIDENTIAL BID

Elizabeth Warren was the first major candidate to enter the 2020 primary race for president, and her campaign message got lost in the negative press surrounding questions around her Native American ancestry. Her commitment to well-conceived and written plans and her devotion to a strong organization, as well as her energetic campaigning, drew significant attention to her campaign and helped to distinguish her when other candidates were infighting or less active on the trail. She seemed the candidate to beat in summer 2019; that was evidenced on the debate stage, especially in the second debate, when her opponents seemed to go after her more than they did any other candidate. She was totally on message until she wasn't—and that lapse occurred when a group of her rivals voiced sharp skepticism of her agenda or accused her of taking impractical stances on issues like health care and taxation. Most notable among these was Amy Klobuchar, who called Warren's platform a "pipe dream."[24] When Warren stopped calling for "Medicare for All," her opponents claimed she was flip-flopping.

The overall sense that she could not beat Trump kept emerging as a theme. Haunted by the "E" word—electability—she began in her speeches to speak to the perception that she was not electable. Perhaps she addressed this too obliquely when she argued that the country's best moments were when it could turn "despair into hope, fear into courage, improbability into triumph."[25] But she also came right out and said, "I believe I would be a better president than Bernie [Sanders]."[26] That assertion was perhaps an attempt to rise above him in the polls and to put herself into the same sentence as president in the minds of the voters, again trying to quell the perception that she was not electable.

Warren was a presidential candidate who electrified her audiences with a roll-up-your-sleeves message that reminded her supporters to dream big and to fight hard. She did so with energy and enthusiasm. The early lesson she learned from her mother, who took a minimum-wage job at Sears to save the family home, was one she brought to her presidential campaign. She said as much when she told her audience in Arizona: "I felt that is the lesson my mama taught me, and that is: No matter how hard it looks, no matter how scared you are, what it comes down to is, you reach down deep, you find what you have to find, you pull it up, and you take care of the people you love."[27] The underlying message was that you have to do what you have to do to reach your goals, whether it is keeping your family afloat or running for president.

AFTER HER PRESIDENTIAL BID

Elizabeth Warren returned to her work in the Senate and continued to work as an insurgent, trying to answer the fundamental question that has been the driving force of her professional career: Why do Americans go broke? With the dramatic downward turn of the economy brought on by the Covid-19 virus, it is likely that her research into this topic will serve the United States especially well. She brought her own family's experience—the loss of her oldest brother to her rhetoric on Covid-19—and blamed the Trump administration for acting too slowly in the beginning of the pandemic, letting the virus get out of hand in a way that, she argued, with better leadership, never would have happened. She has a personal story that many in the United States can related to, and that is very much to her advantage. She now has great name recognition, also to her advantage, because a candidate needs broad support to win the U.S. presidency. As she told the large crowd gathered at a Working Families Party rally in New York City in September 2019 as she campaigned for the presidency, "I never thought I'd get into politics, not in a million years, but when I got into this fight, I quickly found out nobody makes it on their own. If you're going to make any kind of progress in this country, you need allies who know how to fight."[28] To realize her vision for the middle class in America, Elizabeth Warren will need to gain the support of a wider coalition than her Massachusetts home state. Will she run again? Time will tell.

Warren was easily the most prepared candidate who garnered much attention early on in the 2020 primary race for her well-researched and written plans. But today's political climate does not seem to reward the most intellectual, carefully coordinated candidate; in addition, her political leanings may have been too far left for the majority of voters, who eventually nominated a moderate white male, Joe Biden, who had been in U.S. politics more than forty years. There is cause to wonder whether U.S. voters will ever consider a woman over seventy (like Warren) able to compete against male candidates in the same age range—as both Joe Biden and Donald Trump are in 2020.

Elizabeth Warren was still very much on the mind of President Trump when he debated Joe Biden in late September 2020, referring to her with his derisive nickname, Pocahontas, in one of the least civil political debates of modern times. Perhaps President Trump was thinking about how sharply her rhetorical skills would have been deployed that evening. Something about the fierce rhetoric and indefatigable, well-organized campaigning that Warren offered early in 2020 suggests she is not finished on the national stage. She changed presidential rhetoric by proving that it is possible not only for a man to extend his career as a national politician beyond age sixty-five but also for a woman to connect with a considerable audience of supporters, including many young campaigners who found her earnest desire to help the middle class succeed appealing.

NOTES

    1. Congressional Record, February 6, 2017. https://www.congress.gov/crec/2017/02/06/CREC-2017-02-06-bk2.pdf (accessed April 21, 2020).

2. Elizabeth Warren's 2020 announcement speech, https://www.masslive.com/politics/2019/02/read-elizabeth-warrens-2020-announcement-speech.html (accessed July 17, 2019).

3. Maggie Kennedy, phone interview with Nichola Gutgold, April 20, 2020.

4. Emily Jacobs, "Bloomberg claimed he 'didn't realize' Warren was still running," *New York Post*, March 3, 2020. https://nypost.com/2020/03/03/bloomberg-claimed-he-didnt-realize-warren-was-still-running/ (accessed March 3, 2020).

5. Seema Mehta, Michael Finnegan and Melanie Mason, "Elizabeth Warren says Bernie Sanders told her a woman couldn't win the presidency," *Los Angeles Times*, https://www.latimes.com/politics/story/2020-01-13/bernie-sanders-elizabeth-warren-campaigns-on-the-attack (accessed January 14, 2020).

6. Steve Peoples, Meg Kinnard and Bill Barrow, "Dem Candidates Attach Bloomberg, Sanders in Debate," *The Arizona Republic*, February 26, 2020, A-1.

7. Dolly Parton, "9-5 lyrics" https://genius.com/Dolly-parton-9-to-5-lyrics (accessed January 2, 2020).

8. Elizabeth Warren, New York City rally speech, September 16, 2020. https://awpc.cattcenter.iastate.edu/2019/09/20/new-york-city-rally-sept-16-2019/ (accessed June 2, 2020).

9. Elizabeth Warren and Amelia Warren Tyagi, *All Your Worth: The Ultimate Lifetime Money Plan* (New York: Simon and Schuster, 2005), 6.

10. Warren, *This Fight Is Our Fight*, 217.

11. Thomas Kaplan, "Warren's Slam on Delaney Was Called the Line of the Night. Here's What She Said," *The New York Times*, July 31, 2019, https://www.nytimes.com/2019/07/30/us/politics/elizabeth-warren-debate.html (accessed July 31, 2019).

12. Ashley Feinberg, "Bloomberg on Being Accused of Sexual Harassment: They Didn't Like a Joke I Told," *Slate*, February 19, 2020, https://slate.com/news-and-politics/2020/02/bloomberg-on-being-accused-of-sexual-harassment-the-didnt-like-a-joke-i-told.html (accessed June 9, 2020).

13. Ibid.

14. Maggie Kennedy, email correspondence with Nichola Gutgold, April 21, 2020.

15. Elena Moore, "Elizabeth Warren Backs Biden, Extending Display of Party Unity," NPR, April 15, 2020, www.npr.org (accessed April 15, 2020).

16. Ali Vitali and Sahil Kapur, "Elizabeth Warren Suspends Her Campaign," NBC, March 5, 2020, https://www.nbcnews.com/politics/2020-election/elizabeth-warren-ends-presidential-run-n1150436 (accessed March 5, 2020).

17. Jacqueline Thomsen, "Donald Trump: Don't Obsess Over My Genes," *The Hill*, July 5, 2018, https://thehill.com/homenews/senate/395736-warren-fires-back-at-trump-dont-obsess-over-my-genes (accessed June 11, 2020).

18. Shane Goldmacher, "Elizabeth Warren: A Populist for the Professional Class," *The New York Times*, https://www.nytimes.com/2020/03/03/us/politics/elizabeth-warren-super-tuesday.html?action=click&module=Top%20Stories&pgtype=Homepage.

19. Jennifer Medina, "They Saw Themselves in Elizabeth Warren. So What Do They See Now?" *The New York Times*, https://www.nytimes.com/2020/02/28/us/

politics/elizabeth-warren-women-voters.html?action=click&module=Top%20Stories &pgtype=Homepage (accessed February 27, 2020).

20. Shane Goldmacher, "She Has A Plan For Telephoning Early and Often," *The New York Times*, December 28, 2019. A-1.

21. Shame Goldmacher and Astead W. Herndon, "Warren's Plan for Bankruptcy Law Recalls Clash in Senate with Biden," *The New York Times*, January 8, 2020, A14.

22. Jaffe, Alexandra, "Buttigieg, Sanders campaigns request Iowa caucus recanvass." Arizona Republican, February 3, 2020, A-1.

23. Maggie Kennedy, phone interview with Nichola Gutgold, April 20, 2020.

24. Katherine Zraick, "Amy Klobuchar Goes After Elizabeth Warren," *The New York Times*, October 16, 2019. https://www.nytimes.com/2019/10/15/us/politics/amy -klobuchar-elizabeth-warren-debate.html (accessed June 11, 2020).

25. Elizabeth Warren, New Year's Eve speech in Boston, Massachusetts, December 31, 2019. ElizabethWarren.com https://2020.elizabethwarren.com/live/nye -speech (accessed April 22, 2020).

26. "Elizabeth Warren: I Would Make a Better President Than Bernie," *The Week*, https://theweek.com/speedreads/898156/elizabeth-warren-make-better-president-than-bernie (accessed June 11, 2020).

27. Peter Marks, "Elizabethan: Warren knows the power of words," *The Washington Post*, August 21, 2019, https://www.washingtonpost.com/arts-entertainment/2019/08/21/posts-theater-critic-is-reviewing-performances-democratic-candidates-this-installment-elizabeth-warren-cuts-shakespearean-figure-arizona/?arc404 =true (accessed September 23, 2020).

28. Elizabeth Warren, New York City rally speech, September 16, 2020, https:// awpc.cattcenter.iastate.edu/2019/09/20/new-york-city-rally-sept-16-2019/ (accessed June 2, 2020).

29 Elizabeth Warren, 2020 campaign announcement speech, Carrie Chapman Catt Center for Women and Politics, Iowa State University.

Chapter 6

Marianne Williamson

Running with the People to Create Deep Change

"Only outrageous truth can beat outrageous lies," Marianne Williamson declared after raising more than $3 million to keep her presidential campaign going. "What guides my life is what guides the life of most people's lives, and that's my conscience and my heart." She went on to say that "the problem we have is the basic divergence of that. We have to close the gap, and that is a moral repair. It is not only what my campaign stands for, it is what my presidency would stand for."[1]

She delivered these remarks with an unflinching, calm persona that assured her audience that she was convinced that she would win. Despite her low polling numbers, she communicated a calm confidence that suggested the campaign would turn in her favor, no matter what the so-called experts said. Still holding firm to her belief in a positive outcome, she laid off her paid staff at the beginning of 2020, citing financial reasons, but vowing that her campaign would continue with a volunteer staff.[2] She officially suspended her campaign on January 10, 2020.

How do most people decide that the time is right to run for president? Historically, most politicians run for president after they've served a number of years in the public eye as senators, in Congress, or as governors, and have come to believe that the time is right for them to move to a larger political stage.

But in 2016, Donald Trump upended the traditional path to the presidency when he proved that you need not be a seasoned politician to not only run for president but also to win. Like Trump, and another 2020 presidential hopeful, Andrew Yang, Marianne Williamson—a best-selling author—had never been elected to a political office when she threw her hat in the presidential ring in 2019. Her message of love and moral conviction, the complete opposite of Trump's, harked back to her spiritual preaching. When reflecting on her decision to get into the race, she said, "It was almost as though I could hear the spirit of my late father: 'This must not go unanswered.'" It was not the first time that Williamson had run for political office. In 2013 she ran for Congress in California's 33rd congressional district. Despite her best efforts, she came in fourth—but she learned an important lesson from the race. As she noted later to Oprah Winfrey, "It taught me what I should have already known: To only listen to myself."[3]

Not surprisingly, Williamson's call to run for president sounds a bit like the "inner dictation" that Helen Schucman, a professor of medical psychology at Columbia University College of Physicians and Surgeons, claimed to experience when writing *A Course In Miracles* (the mystical text, which Schucman claimed was based on new revelations from Jesus Christ himself, would shape the course of Williamson's life and career). For Williamson, her late father's voice coming to her was her impetus, the rhetorical situation that would motivate her to speak out as a political candidate and "show up in a way we've never shown up before."[4] Many of Williamson's campaign speeches and public statements have a sermon-like quality to them. Her many years as a spiritual guide to millions, as well as to some very famous people, gave her messages a fluency that is evident in her writings and presentations. Williamson is a polished, captivating, confident speaker.

Many of Williamson's best-selling books are an extension or popularizing of the teachings of *A Course In Miracles*. In one of them, *The Age of Miracles*, Williamson contends that "we are all born carrying a promise—a promise to make the world better—and there's a yearning to make good on that promise that none of us can suppress forever."[5] It is this same sentiment of action that Williamson explains was the impetus for her presidential run. Williamson's announcement as a presidential candidate was likely the snowball effect of three things: The first factor was real estate mogul and reality TV star Donald Trump's surprising victory in the 2016 presidency. The second was women's entrance into political life in larger numbers than ever before. The third was the input of many Williamson supporters and followers, who noted that she had served as an adviser to many high-level celebrities and presidents and suggested that perhaps it was time she harness the convictions she so long shared with others to lead the country as president.

As early as 2010, politics was clearly on Williamson's mind; she felt her spiritual teachings could help more women become elected. It was the year she participated in a program, hosted by Yale Campaign School, called "Sister Giant."[6] A series of conferences at Yale University, "Sister Giant" was aimed at encouraging more women to run for political office. Williamson's message resonated not only with the hundreds of women who attended; she also took it to heart herself.

Long before she ran for president, Williamson wrote, "It is time to redesign the world—not along traditional economic geopolitical lines, but along deeply humanitarian ones—in which the amelioration of unnecessary human suffering becomes the new organizing principle of human civilization."[7] This core belief, that the country is like a human body that can be made better and could even thrive with proper thinking and care, is one she would bring to her speeches.

When Shirley Chisholm campaigned for president in 1972, she was met with incredulous audiences who questioned what in the world made her think she could run for president. Williamson too, was often interviewed with a snide snicker or was stared at in disbelief. Often she was invited to "explain yourself"[8]—as did the women of the television show "The View"—who also went further by suggesting that her run for president was just an attempt to sell more books. Donald Trump too was treated in the early stages of his 2016 presidential campaign as a complete novelty and surely an impossibility for the presidency. The similarities are easy to point out: Both Trump and Williamson ran for president as celebrity candidates, holding ideas that seemed out of the mainstream. But right there the similarities ended. Williamson's candidacy, based on humanistic connection, seemed as far away as could be imagined from the law-and-order presidency that Trump promised.

Explaining herself and her out-of-the-box ideas seemed to come easily to Williamson. Using the slogan, "Defeat Big Lies with Big Truth," she called on her supporters to change "the economic bottom line to an ethical bottom line."[9] She had put her thoughts into more than a dozen books, and yet, despite that impressive publishing history, most Americans had never heard of Williamson when she announced her bid for the presidency. That was a distinct disadvantage. However, she was effective in transmitting her inspired and unusual message to many Americans—even if they didn't completely understand it—who were watching her on the debate stage and perhaps seeing her for the first time. Her message was not too dissimilar from former vice president Joseph R. Biden Jr.'s pledge to re-claim the "soul of America"—so why did her campaign provide so much fodder for ridicule by late-night comedians? This chapter will offer an analysis of Williamson's presidential bid and attempt to answer this question.

The overarching theme of Marianne Williamson's race for president is that we need to be brave, because we've faced challenging hardships before, and we can overcome all our problems with "decency and a commitment to human values and the actual tenets and traditions of American democracy."[10] In the first Democratic debate, she expressed her view when she addressed President Donald Trump directly in her concluding remarks:

I'm sorry we haven't talked more tonight about how we're going to beat Donald Trump. I have an idea about Donald Trump: Donald Trump is not going to be beaten just by insider politics talk. He's not going to be beaten just by somebody who has plans. He's going to be beaten by somebody who has an idea what the man has done. This man has reached into the psyche of the American people and he has harnessed fear for political purposes.

So, Mr. President—if you're listening—I want you to hear me please: You have harnessed fear for political purposes and only love can cast that out. So I, sir, I have a feeling you know what you're doing. I'm going to harness love for political purposes. I will meet you on that field, and sir, love will win.[11]

BEST-SELLING AUTHOR AND SPIRITUAL GURU

Marianne Williamson is a native of Houston, Texas, and the youngest of three children of Samuel Williamson, an immigration lawyer, whom she refers to often in her political campaign memoir, *A Politics of Love*, and Sophie Ann (Kaplan), a homemaker.

By all accounts, she lived a fairly privileged and somewhat unorthodox childhood. Her parents were world travelers, who took Marianne and her siblings traveling with them around the world when they were children. The travel shaped her in ways she reflected upon later: "The fact that I traveled internationally at such a young age made me a different person than I would otherwise have become. I learned very early, with the clarity of a child, that everyone deep down is the same." She also noted, "While I didn't realize it growing up, as an adult I have come to recognize the impeccable ethics and values that were demonstrated to me as a child." She notes that she was made "deeply aware of issues of social justice" mainly because her father grew up in poverty and wanted the children to realize how fortunate they were.

She went to public schools in Houston, and spent two years at Pomona College in Claremont, California. She had a deep sense of social justice and felt a strong pull toward the social revolution of the 1960s. On her presidential website she says she "went on to experience pretty much every outwardly insignificant thing and every inwardly profound thing that's possible."[12]

She explains how her path to self-help emerged:

The most consistent thing about my early twenties was a search for spiritual understanding. I had a voracious appetite for topics of comparative religion and philosophy, and in my mid-20's I began reading a set of books called *A Course in Miracles*. The *Course* is not a religion, but rather a self-study program of spiritual psychotherapy based on universal spiritual themes. There is no dogma or doctrine; it is simply a book on how to forgive. I had no idea at the time that my study of *The Course*, plus writing and speaking about it, would turn into a 35-year career.

She became very popular as a spiritual guide to celebrities. Her books and lectures have reached millions.[13] During the HIV/AIDS crisis, she provided counseling and food to patients in Los Angeles. Her first book, *A Return to Love: Reflections on the Principles of "A Course in Miracles,"* was featured on The Oprah Winfrey Show. Williamson has since written a dozen more books and gained an international following. In 2014 when Williamson ran as an independent in California's 33rd congressional district, she lost with 13.2 percent of the vote.

Her platform included paying reparations to the descendants of slaves, overhauling the public education system, and combating climate change. She has said that the country needs to "wage peace" instead of investing in preparation for war. She supports progressive policies like "Medicare for All" and the Green New Deal.

In 1989, she founded Project Angel Food, a meals-on-wheels program that serves homebound people with AIDS in the Los Angeles area. She has remarked that gay men gave her her career, insofar as it focused her work on ministry and spirituality.

RHETORIC OF WILLIAMSON'S PRESIDENTIAL RACE

Her overarching goal as president would be to search for "higher wisdom" to lead the country. According to her presidential campaign website,

> There is a groundswell of people in America who are seeking higher wisdom. We are rich and poor, progressive and conservative, young and old. And what we share at this moment is deep concern—concern about the direction in which our country is headed, the assaults on our democratic foundations, and the erosion of our human values.[14]

Her rhetoric is wide-ranging. While she holds specific views on a number of important campaign issues, her speeches and interviews are mostly focused on a campaign of peace and love. The structure of her rhetoric is a broad view of the main societal ills and a conviction that to get the country on a better path, we need a completely new way to look at its needs.

In Williamson's presidential video announcement, she appears as a talking head in front of a window with plants. In an almost whispered tone, she says, "Hi, I'm Marianne Williamson and I'm considering running as a candidate for the Democratic nomination for the presidency in 2020 and I'm going to tell you why." She says that "we had a miracle in this country in 1776 and we need one now."[15] Citing the well-known Abraham Lincoln quote that a government "of the people, by the people and for the people shall not perish from the earth," she takes issue with Lincoln's statement: while the pace of her speech is often quite fast, she says slowly, for emphasis, "It is perishing now."[16] She lays out her main argument: because America is in a state of crisis, it needs a leader who knows how to deal with crisis.

She reminds the listener that American people are problem-solvers. While we have faced great challenges in the past such as slavery, the oppression of women, and white supremacy, she continues, movements have always come forward to take on and overcome those challenges. She suggests optimistically that this is another time in history where we all have to band together to create the solution to the dire circumstances in America that the policies of the Trump administration have perpetuated. She says we need to come forward and push back against a government that is not in line with our ethical values. "We have to get back to our ethical center that is the true exceptionalism of our nation,"[17] she says.

Williamson's career as a self-help author comes through in her campaign book *A Politics of Love*, where she likens the state of the country to a body that is sick and out of alignment. She writes, "Just as the body has an immune system, so does a society. Just as cells awaken to the need to heal an injured body, citizens awaken to the need to heal an injured group."[18]

In the second Democratic primary debate, Williamson stood out for her articulate and clear responses, which were strong on specifics, especially in terms of race relations. If critics of her first performance cast her as an aging hippie with a free-love message, her "sharp answers on race relations"[19] in the second debate showed her ability to respond to critics and the country's needs. She called for more than a change in thinking, proposing the enactment of laws that would fundamentally change how we deal with people. At the same time, Williamson stayed true to her holistically feminine approach to the world's problems. When responding to a question on reparations for slavery, she said, "It's not $500 billion in financial assistance, it's a $200 to $500 billion payment of a debt that is owed. . . . We need deep truth-telling when it comes, we don't need another commission to look at evidence." She added,

I appreciate what Congressman [Beto] O'Rourke has said. It is time for us to simply realize that this country will not heal. All that a country is, is a collection of people. People heal when there's some deep truth-telling. We need to recognize, when it comes to the economic gap between Blacks and whites in America, it does come from a great injustice that has never been dealt with. That great injustice has had to do with the fact that there was 250 years of slavery followed by another hundred years of domestic terrorism.[20]

In classical rhetoric, "invention" is the art of choosing the appropriate arguments for a given rhetorical situation. When Williamson chooses her arguments, she most often includes the moral issues facing America; how she can help America experience the same spiritual awakening she experienced in order to create a culture based on love; and why, fundamentally, most people want the same thing: health, wealth, equality, love, and education.

One aspect of Williamson's ethos is how her unique upbringing shaped her worldview and taught her to really see the true challenges that society faces. She particularly credits her father for trying to offer her and her siblings a chance to become more globally aware. He would organize international trips that would take her family to witness firsthand different cultures and the struggles that face various cultures. According to Williamson, these travel experiences made her realize that deep down no matter how different people may seem, in actuality they are not very different. She offers an example, quoting her father:

> "Kids, come here. Let me tell you what's really going on here." And that's why my father always was—my father was even someone when the teacher told me in the seventh grade, I came home and told my family told my parents that the teacher had said, my social studies teacher said that "We have to fight in Vietnam, because if we don't fight in Vietnam, we will be fighting on the shores of Hawaii. It was called the domino theory." I said. My father stood up, he said, "Sweetheart," to my mother, "get the visas, we're going to Vietnam."[21]

The themes of Williamson's speeches include income inequality, traumatized children, money and politics, suffering, medicine, empathy, and compassion. In a 2019 speech at the Iowa State Fair, she linked the economy and education to a lack of value alignment, suggesting that the current political structure serves only to perpetuate the economic and educational issues in America. She argues that only through the rising of people power and love from the people—not government—can these destructive policies be reversed.

> Our politics are stuck in the twentieth century, but our love is in the twenty-first century. We have a real problem on our hands, ladies and gentlemen, and that is, our politics are not aligned with our deep goodness. Tax policies which make it easier for rich people to get rich and make it harder for everyone else to even make it. That's not aligned with our goodness. Policies that stay in place so that millions of American children live with chronic trauma—so that millions of American children go to school every day in classrooms that don't even have the adequate school supplies with which to teach a child to read, and yes, those children are in Iowa, too. And if a child doesn't learn to read by that age of eight, the chances of high school graduation is drastically decreased, and the chances of incarceration are significantly increased.[22]

Most often, Williamson will use a combination of topical and historical ordering of main points for the disposition or organization of her speeches. She draws from history to provide proof that her strategy for improving the country will work.

Perhaps because her core message of greater morality and love has been constant throughout her thirty-year career, Marianne Williamson speaks often without notes, from memory, in a polished and professional manner. She never seems to become flustered and doesn't seem to take offense when asked about her qualifications. This calm command of her audiences no doubt has risen from her many years as a motivational speaker. She is so firmly rooted in her belief system, so polished and prepared, that she does not become flustered.

At a CNN Town Hall meeting in April 2019, Olivia Mugenga, a law student at Howard University, pointedly asked Williamson, "While your call to healing America is touching, what is the political knowledge that you bring to the scene? What experience do you have that makes you fit to lead this great nation?"[23] Calmly, no doubt having anticipated this question, Williamson said:

> You know, the Latin root of the word "politeia" doesn't mean of the government. It means of the people. And I think our political establishment has gotten too far away from the people. We have a political establishment that doesn't get to the heart of the matter, doesn't speak to what's really wrong. Politicians don't really get down and talk about what's really wrong, even though they know it. And because they don't talk about what's really wrong, they don't get to what can really be made within us. So in a way, for me, I challenge the idea that people whose careers have been entrenched in the same limitations that are endemic to the system that got us into this ditch are the only people we should possibly consider qualified to take us out of the ditch. I challenge that, and that's why I'm running.[24]

Dana Bash, the host, followed up and asked Williamson, "You have said, and we know that you have a career in inspiring action inside people. And you've said that that gives you a unique qualification or set of qualifications for the presidency. But as you well know, being president is more than inspiring people, so running a government, that particular qualification, why do think you have that?"

Again, Williamson was calm and composed as she answered:

> You know, Dana, as you well know, what has happened in this country didn't come out of nowhere, and we have a crisis in our democracy. And that crisis is due to the fact that we've been sliding for the last forty years away from

democracy and into aristocracy, because of tax policies, because of corporate subsidies, because of the nefarious influence of money on our political system. We have gone from a system where we prize, as we should, in an economic as well as political democracy, equal opportunity for everyone to a situation where a small group of people—this is what we repudiated in 1776. You don't have to be a politician to get this. And sometimes I think everybody else gets it more than the politicians do. We repudiated an aristocracy in 1776. We repudiated a situation in which only a small group of people are entitled to the major resources of a country. We repudiated the idea of a government advocating for a small group of people as opposed to everyone else, and we need to repudiate [it] again. I'm running because the politicians aren't doing it. My qualification, if anything, is that I'll name what everybody knows and apparently they won't name.[25]

Presidential candidate Marianne Williamson heaped criticism on the Democratic Party in the fourth Democratic debate, saying President Trump would be reelected if Democratic candidates continued to use the same tactics against him.

"The Democratic Party is in such a state of denial, I'm afraid. There is no conversation of any depth or reality about what the president represents and what it's going to take to defeat him," Williamson warned on MSNBC. "This idea that we all just need to come together around the values. What, the values of health care? We're forgetting who this man is. This president is not just a politician, he is a phenomenon. The Democrats are sharpening their knives and he will be bringing a gun to this battle."

Williamson, who did not qualify for the debate, went on to warn her listeners that Donald Trump would be the same person that he was when he first ran in 2016, but "on steroids" in the 2020 race because he would have the benefit of being the incumbent and the "power of the Russians with him for all we know." Regarding what it will take to beat Trump in 2020, Williamson said, "Well, I'm doing it by having a completely different conversation. He is a reality show. I'm showing reality. And the Democratic establishment is just coming with the same sort of twentieth-century conversation. It didn't excite people last time."[26] She warned that many Americans watching the debate must be thinking, "I think we are in trouble here."[27]

Williamson went on to encourage everyone to vote in the next election and to be serious about how challenging it will be to beat Trump. Her rhetoric stressed the importance of "knowing our place in history going backwards and going forwards. People are hungry for deeper understanding."[28]

Media Frames

Marianne Williamson is often portrayed as an aging hippie with unconventional ideas.

There was a lot of fun made of her. But then, after the second debate, she became the second most Googled candidate, because she was a polished and prepared communicator. She appeared utterly confident and self-assured about her message and what she could offer the country as president. Yet, as the primary election season went on, she continued to poll at the very bottom of the candidates. Of all the women who ran for president in 2020, Williamson received a disproportionate amount of misogyny and agism. When male candidates quote Lincoln and call for a return to decency they are lauded. Williamson's credibility suffered because she was often portrayed as a political neophyte who was espousing mysticism, when in reality her views were similar to Robert Kennedy and Martin Luther King Jr.'s messages of unity.

Marianne Williamson's Public Speaking

Marianne Williamson is a mesmerizing, soothing, and captivating public speaker. She speaks quickly and almost breathlessly, yet in a very smooth and consistent way. She has given hundreds of speeches over the years and her polished style is evident. Her almost forty-year career as a speaker is evident in how she unflinchingly responds to challenges.

Invention

Williamson's public speaking has been consistent, because she unfailingly took her life-coaching approach to heal the country's ailments. She was able to make a complete, holistic parallel between healing people over the years and prescribing a healing approach to the United States. She wrote her own speeches, often committed them to memory and delivered them in a rhythmic, assured style.

Disposition

Marianne Williamson organized her speeches by offering historical examples that related to today's issues in society. She often organized her speeches in a chronological format, showing how different groups of people have overcome many challenges over the history of the country. She cited civil rights leaders and suffragists who had to battle for their freedoms, reassuring the American people that they have to be brave like our foremothers and forefathers and step up to the challenges at hand. She quoted Hitler by saying that

"The only way they could have gotten us is if they came after us early, swift and hard."[29]

Style

Marianne Williamson's use of language in her speeches—her rhetorical style—has a number of unique characteristics. She uses history as an example more so than her own life, unlike a number of her contemporary female counterparts. Her use of the active voice to recount historical lessons gives her public speaking urgency, passion and energy. While Joe Biden adopted the mantra saving "the soul of the nation," it was Marianne Williamson's use of this rhetorical style—to talk to people instead of about them—that stood out as a unique rhetorical style early in the presidential primary campaign. It was a message that she shared long before her political aspirations were realized by running for office. Her life's work has been about healing, and her argument—that the nation is like a body in dis-ease, is one that was uniquely hers at first. This style of speaking seems completely authentic to Williamson because perhaps it is an extension of her work as a motivational speaker who has consistently written and spoken about self-improvement and spiritual issues to make life better for her audiences.

Delivery

Marianne Williamson delivers her speeches with the flawless precision of a trained actor. She is attractive and slim, with well-cut suits and perfectly styled hair. She seemed to enjoy public speaking and often smiles and nods, moving freely on stage and using her arms and hands to demonstrate her points. Williamson is a comfortable, high-energy composed speaker who is in complete control of her material.

Memoria

Marianne Williamson rarely speaks from notes. Unlike many speakers who do not speak from notes, she does not ramble; even without a script, note cards, or a teleprompter, she is well organized. Because her messages are informed by her core beliefs, she speaks fluently and without pause. Williamson believes that seeing the good in others and applying love to our country are both essential. She speaks without hesitation, calling on the country to love fiercely in order to confront the hate in the world—because she believes that what ails the country is a lack of spiritual integrity. She underscores the shortcomings of American politics, arguing that politicians focus too much on symptoms of U.S. problems and too little their causes.

She uses many stories and lessons to illustrate her basic tenet that while most people are good, we have stopped defending our democracy. Her core point is that while people are essentially good, the Democratic system is broken and in need of repair. The only way we can repair it, she says, is to vote Donald Trump out of office. Perhaps because her core message of greater morality and love has been constant throughout her thirty-year career, Marianne Williamson speaks often without notes, from memory, in a polished and professional manner. She never seems to become flustered and doesn't seem to take offense when asked about her qualifications. This calm command of her audiences no doubt has risen from her many years as a motivational speaker. She is so firmly rooted in her belief system, so polished and prepared, that she does not become flustered.

OBSTACLES TO PRESIDENTIAL BID

Previous to the 2016 election, it would have been easy to say that a major political obstacle to being president was never having held political office. But since America elected Donald Trump, who lacked previous political experience, that can no longer be said. And yet, for women candidates in particular, it seems the electorate wants them to have more credentials, not fewer. During Marianne Williamson's race for the presidency, the press seemed barely able to hold back all-out laughter at her bid. the *New York Times* columnist David Brooks called her ideas "wack-a-doodle," and CNN anchor Anderson Cooper asked her who she planned to support in the race—even though she herself was a candidate. Leaving Williamson out of a *Vogue* cover shot was just one of the many ways the press tried to erase her as a presidential contender. While there was a lot of tolerance for Donald Trump's lack of political experience, Williamson was constantly called on her lack of political experience—demonstrating how her gender inhibited her run for president.

Repeatedly questioned about her lack of political experience, she often responded in this way: "We need more than new policies. We need a new worldview. We need to replace economic values with humanitarian values as an ordering principle."[30] Another point of contention was created by previous statements Williamson made about mandatory vaccinations being "draconian" and "Orwellian"—statements she later walked back and apologized for. Further, CNN's Anderson Cooper asked her about her questioning of the use of anti-depressant drugs. She defended herself by saying that while issues like "normal human despair" and "grief" have traditionally been aided by religion and spirituality, over the last few years the baton has been passed over to psychopharmacology. In a tweet and elsewhere, Williamson had indicated that too many Americans were "numbing our pain" with anti-depressants. Cooper noted that Williamson had called clinical depression "a scam" in a podcast with British comedian and actor Russell Brand. But Williamson pointed out that her stance on anti-depressants, like so many of her positions, had been mischaracterized. Marianne Williamson has had to consistently fight off the critics and people laughing at her as she attempted to share her views. But she did not cower or flinch. She simply presented her views earnestly.

AFTER HER PRESIDENTIAL BID

The passionate urgency with which Marianne Williamson urged voters to see the bigger picture and to understand that the 2020 race is about a moral awakening, made her well-known far beyond her reach as an author and spiritual guru. Despite her low showing in the polls, there is evidence that her message was influential to at least one Democratic front-runner (Joe Biden), who began to argue that his campaign was for the "soul of America."

In the conclusion of her book, *The Age of Miracles*, Williamson writes of her overall vision for society in a style that closely resembles her rhetoric as a presidential candidate. She says, "It is the ultimate goal here: the birth of a new humanity."[31] She was calling for a paradigm shift for all of America.

On January 10, 2020, Marianne Williamson suspended her campaign for president. In a heartfelt letter she thanked all her supporters and campaign workers and ended with "A politics of conscience is still yet possible. And yes . . . love *will* prevail."[32]

Although Marianne Williamson suspended her presidential campaign in January 2020, Marianne Williamson is still working on her ultimate goal for the United States through her speeches, writings and teachings. It is clear that long before Marianne Williamson decided to run for president of the United States, she was thinking, writing, and speaking about how the world could be improved by humanity-focused spiritualty. "Politics and economics have to mirror our spirituality or else they mock it."[33]

In the conclusion of her campaign book, A Politics of Love, she puts her call to action more urgently: "The day has come for an American reckoning. This is not the time to close our eyes, but to open them to the light within. It is a time of atonement, a time of replanting, and a time of deliverance. Or not; the choice is ours. In honor of our ancestors, and in honor of our descendants, may we choose well. May we choose wisely. May we choose love.[34] While Williamson's message as a presidential candidate caught many by surprise, it is not an unprecedented message from a leader. Many of her words and calls to action are reminiscent of Bobby Kennedy and Martin Luther King Jr., who asked Americans to call for peace and love and to consider an overall new paradigm for America, one based on human dignity and a call to consider future generations.

Shortly after her exit from presidential politics, Williamson held a conference to discuss major issues facing Americans. "Americans sometimes have an odd idea about what makes up failure and what makes up success," she said. "My effort failed as a presidential campaign, but it succeeded in putting a lot of ideas out there that I feel belong in the national debate."[35]

As Bernie Sanders showed early success in the Iowa caucus, New Hampshire primary, and Nevada caucus, Williamson endorsed him, saying, "Bernie Sanders has taken a stand! And he has taken a stand for a long time! He has been consistent. He has been connected. He has been committed!"[36]

After Joe Biden was chosen as the Democratic nominee for president, Williamson continued to speak out about the U.S. democracy. She was interviewed by Sally Quinn at *The Washington Post*, who fielded a question from a listener who asked Williamson what she learned from running for president. She said, "I learned two main categories of things. The system of running for president is more corrupt than I even knew and that the intelligence, dignity and decency of the American voters is even more than I had hoped."[37]

She said that these diametrically opposed takeaways reflect what is wrong with the country's political process, adding that President Trump was harnessing collectivized racism for political gain. She urged listeners to read history and to identify with people who have helped solve problems throughout the years. She believes that the country needs to fear nothing and love everything. She will likely continue to speak out about the core of her political and spiritual beliefs: that love is the ultimate political rebellion. We will not let despair defeat us. You will not get my democracy on my watch. She forcefully urged listeners to get involved, saying, "We have to be committed behind our love. We are serious about our democracy."[38] Williamson is not sure she will run for president again. "When I talked to voters," she said, "there was definitely a connection, but media smears that made me seem silly hurt my image and made a lot of people think that they were too serious to come to hear me. But I wasn't characterized as silly because I was silly, they characterized me as silly because I was resonating with voters."[39] Marianne Williamson changed presidential politics for women because the thinking has always been that women need to be governors or at least senators to be considered qualified. And yet, there was Williamson, speaking with the wish to save the soul of America, the mantra adopted by none other than the future president of the United States, Joe Biden.

NOTES

1. Marianne Williamson, live interview on CNN, November 9, 2019.

2. John DiStaso, "Democrat Marianne Williamson lays off campaign staff nationally, including NH," WMUR, January 3, 2020. https://www.wmur.com/

article/democrat-marianne-williamson-lays-off-campaign-staff-nationally-including -nh/30382582# (accessed January 3, 2020).

3. Oprah Winfrey, Super Soul Sunday, http://www.oprah.com/own-super-soul -sunday/oprah-to-marianne-williamson-how-important-was-the-win-video#ixzz-5W1Tzz8SN (accessed January 3, 2020).

4. Marianne Schnall, *What Will It Take to Make a Woman President?* (Berkeley: Seal Press, 2013), 231.

5. Marianne Williamson, *The Age of Miracles* (New York: Hay House, 2008), 7.

6. Ibid, 171.

7. Alexandra Lett (January 19, 2018). "Marianne Williamson Spreads Message Of Unity" My Daily Record, http://mydailyrecord.com/stories/marianne-williamson -spreads-message-of-unity,4174 (accessed January 3, 2020).

8. Marianne Williamson appears on The View, https://www.youtube.com/watch ?v=t75Y-GdzLIc (accessed July 21, 2019).

9. Video on https://www.marianne2020.com/ website "Defeat Big Lies with Big Truths" accessed January 2, 2020.

10. Nichola D. Gutgold, phone interview with Marianne Williamson, October 16, 2020.

11. Marianne Williamson, closing remarks, Democratic debate, June 27, 2019, "Marianne Williamson's 'girlfriend' call to New Zealand and her other best moments in the debates," *Vox*, https://www.vox.com/policy-and-politics/2019/6/28/18961296/ marianne-williamson-democratic-debate-oprah-meme-twitter (accessed July 17, 2019).

12. Marianne Williamson 2020 website, https://www.marianne2020.com/my -story. (accessed August 27, 2019).

13. Simon Sebag Montefiore, "Marianne Williamson: Who Is She & Why Do We Need Her Now?", *Psychology Today*, July 1, 1992, https://www.psychologytoday .com/us/articles/199207/marianne-williamson-who-is-she-why-do-we-need-her-now (accessed July 21, 2019).

14. Marianne Williamson, Presidential Announcement video, November 15, 2018, published on Marianne Williamson's You Tube channel, https://www.youtube.com/ watch?v=37_NkgOn7-w. (accessed July 22, 2019).

15. Ibid.

16. Ibid.

17. Ibid.

18. Marianne Williamson, *A Politics of Love* (New York: Harper One, 2019), 12.

19. Marianne Williamson Presidential Website, https://www.marianne2020.com/ (accessed September 5, 2019).

20. Nick Corasaniti, "Marianne Williamson on Race, Reparations and Trump's 'Dark Psychic Force,'" *The New York Times,* July 31, 2019, https://www.nytimes .com/2019/07/30/us/politics/marianne-williamson-debate-quotes.html (accessed July 31, 2019).

21. Marianne Williamson, presidential announcement speech, January 28, 2019 https://2020poolreports.substack.com/p/transcript-marianne-williamson-us (accessed September 5, 2019).

22. Marianne Williamson, speech at the Iowa State Fair, https://www.youtube.com/watch?v=gz1M6R6M160 (accessed January 6, 2020).

23. Marianne Williamson, CNN Town Hall, April 14, 2019. https://www.google.com/search?q=democratic+town+hall+dana+bash+and+marianne+williamson&sxsrf=ACYBGNThdNkDuGqui9BNnSQts3e7UUtMHA:1578328094233&tbm=isch&source=iu&ictx=1&fir=VRliTRU7AEojJM%253A%252C_SNPl3rS--QygM%252C_&vet=1&usg=AI4_-kTJutPVF9mBhgc3LndGrIU7yyBvAw&sa=X&ved=2ahUKEwiy85Srsu_mAhUwwFkKHYzbCRkQ9QEwB3oECAkQBg#imgrc=PwrnydpuRZhGNM:&vet=1 (accessed January 6, 2020).

24. Ibid.

25. Ibid.

26. Marianne Williamson, MSNBC, https://www.realclearpolitics.com/video/2019/09/16/marianne_williamson_after_watching_third_democratic_primary_debate_i_thought_we_might_be_in_trouble_here.html (accessed January 6, 2020).

27. Ibid.

28. Nichola D. Gutgold, phone interview with Marianne Williamson, October 16, 2020.

29. Sally Quinn, "A Conversation with Marianne Williamson," *The Washington Post / LIVE*, October 1, 2020 https://www.washingtonpost.com/video/washington-post-live/a-conversation-with-marianne-williamson/2020/10/01/9321d868-8db7-4a23-8732-469db5144619_video.html (accessed October 2, 2020).

30. Schnall, *What Will It Take to Make*, 239.

31. Williamson, *The Age of Miracles*, 181.

32. Marianne Williamson Suspends Her Campaign, Marianne Wililamson campaign website. https://www.marianne2020.com/posts/with-love-and-gratitude (accessed January 10, 2020).

33. Ibid., 173.

34. Williamson, *A Politics of Love*, 228.

35. Jonah Engel Bromwich, "I Quit the Presidential Campaign," *The New York Times*, January 20, 2020, https://www.nytimes.com/2020/01/20/style/marianne-williamson-presidential-race.html (accessed February 15, 2020).

36. Kenneth Garger, "Marianne Williamson Endorses Bernie Sanders After Nevada Vote," *New York Post*, February 23, 2020, https://nypost.com/2020/02/23/marianne-williamson-endorses-bernie-sanders-after-his-nevada-win/ (accessed February 24, 2020).

37. Quinn, "A Conversation with Marianne Williamson."

38. Ibid.

39. Nichola D. Gutgold, phone interview with Marianne Williamson, October 16, 2020.

Conclusion

From Novelty to Normal—Did Six Women Running for President 2020 Change the Rhetoric of Women and Presidential Politics?

In September 2020, when feminist icon and Supreme Court Justice Ruth Bader Ginsburg died, it seemed superficial when President Donald Trump nominated another woman—Amy Coney Barrett, her ideological opposite—to replace her. Presumably she was chosen because, well, Barrett is a woman, too. A similar "replacement" occurred in 1991 when Clarence Thomas was chosen to fill the seat of retiring U.S. Supreme Court justice (and civil rights activist) Thurgood Marshall. Barrett's identity as a woman, and Thomas's as a black man, seemed to play into the idea that anyone of the same gender or race would theoretically make up for the loss. This mistaken idea is one of the perils of identity politics, one that can be overcome when we have more than a handful of women or people of color serving at the highest levels of government. The same wrong-headed observation could be made about the selection of Kamala Harris as the vice presidential nominee—that is, that she was chosen because she is a black woman. To put this outdated and false notion to rest, it is essential that more people of all identities—men, women, black, white, Asian, Latino and more—need to enter the political arena. When that happens, and when we have attained a critical mass of diversity, that situation will be perceived as the norm—it will be seen just as the way it is. As of this writing, the mere presence of a book about women who have run for president shines a light on the paucity of women in political office. But someday—and I hope that day comes soon—this book will be a quaint analysis of a time when society was just awakening to the talents that could serve it best.

Years before the midterm election that brought the Congress to its highest level of women serving (25 percent)—and before six women ran for president in the 2020 primary—Kathleen Dolan, a political science professor at the University of Wisconsin Milwaukee, surveyed voters in races involving women running for Congress and governor. The survey indicated that scholars, journalists and pundits alike over-estimate the centrality of gender to voters in making decisions. Dolan does not go so far as to say that gender does not matter; rather, she found that gender stereotypes "appear to be easing, and general attitudes about women's integration into politics are largely positive or neutral." While some gender stereotypes persist, Dolan found, "attitudes are generally not important to shaping concrete actions such as vote choice."[1]

And yet, after Elizabeth Warren bowed out of the 2020 race, the closest a woman would get to the presidency would be as vice president. Indeed, choosing a woman as a vice presidential candidate is a promise that Joseph R. Biden Jr. delivered upon with his selection of Kamala Harris. Leading up to his decision, there was much speculation about who that woman might be. Democratic congressman James Clyburn of South Carolina, whose hearty endorsement of Biden helped to clinch his presumptive Democratic nominee status, said it was "not a must" for the former vice president to pick a black woman as his running mate. "I think having a woman on the ticket is a must. I'm among those who feel that it would be great for him to select a woman of color. But that is not a must."[2] In addition to Harris and other black women contenders, Biden was reported to have considered Stacey Abrams, the former Georgia gubernatorial candidate. Abrams actively campaigned for the job, saying she would be an "excellent" addition to the ticket. Vice presidential hopefuls have usually displayed a false modesty and even (faux) surprise at being considered. But Abrams, who believed that voter suppression was the reason she lost the governorship of Georgia by a razor-thin margin, explained that she learned that being coy about her ambition was not an effective strategy. "As a young black girl growing up in Mississippi," she said, "I learned that if I didn't speak up for myself, no one else would."[3] U.S. senators Amy Klobuchar, and Elizabeth Warren, as well as Michigan governor Gretchen Whitmer, also surfaced as contenders. Klobuchar, who had fallen from the top of the list in the aftermath of the police brutality that led to the death of George Floyd in her home state of Minnesota, took herself out of the running, urging Biden to choose an African American woman.

Prognosticating that if he won the presidency and would serve only one term, Biden noted that he could be determining the nation's future president by his choice of a running mate. Having now clinched the vice presidential nomination, Harris conceivably will have a clearer pathway to the presidency than any woman previously in the United States. We've had six women vie for the Democratic nomination—and one of the constraints that held them back is their perceived electability. One of the major hurdles to electing a woman president has been that voters cannot picture a woman in executive leadership. Before we elect a woman president, we have to be able to visualize a woman in the Oval Office; vice president is as close as you can get to the presidency without actually *being* president. *Candidate* Joe Biden's vice presidential choice was groundbreaking; Now, as president-elect (as of this writing), that choice has become singularly the largest contribution he could have made to gender parity. As the early-August 2020 date for Biden's big announcement neared, more names of women entered the arena as possible vice presidential candidates. The choice of a woman took on a new shimmer of possibility as a global pandemic competed with race riots sparked by the death of George Floyd for the attention of the world. Elizabeth Warren, and three relatively new names, Keisha Lance Bottoms, Val Demings, and Susan Rice—all women of color—became "seriously considered"[4] for the post. Bottoms has served as the mayor of Atlanta since 2018; as the racial unrest of the nation grew, so did her national profile. Demings has been a U.S. representative from Florida since 2017. Before that, she rose to police chief in Orlando after working for years as a police officer. Her national profile grew when she served as the impeachment manager in the Senate trial of President Trump. Susan Rice served in the Barack Obama administration as national security adviser and ambassador to the United Nations, but she has never run for or served in an elective public office. The name of Karen Bass, U.S. representative from California, also emerged in the weeks leading up to Joe Biden's announcement; that brought to light her trail-blazing status (before joining the U.S. Congress) as the first African American woman to be named speaker of the California Assembly.

In anticipation of Joe Biden's vice presidential pick, a group of influential women composed and signed a memo titled, "We Have Her Back," and addressed it to "News Division Heads, Editors in Chief, Bureau Chiefs, Political Directors, Editors, Producers, Reporters and Anchors." The memo read, "Women have been subject to stereotypes and tropes about qualifications, leadership, looks, relationships and experience. Those stereotypes are often amplified and weaponized for Black and Brown women," they wrote. The diversity and high profiles of the signatories, as well as the proactive and pointed nature of the letter, are unprecedented.[5]

The support for a woman as the vice presidential candidate was buoyed by Women's Media Center, Planned Parenthood, Supermajority, Time's Up, EMILY's List, and Higher Heights for America. These groups, along with other influential organizations, have always focused on supporting women in power and on the ways that women running for office are mistreated by the press. Their support may have worked, and perhaps the nation's rapt attention on the Covid-19 pandemic may have resulted in the gendered coverage of the election and the vice presidential pick of a woman, let alone a woman of color, did not appear to be as much a focus of press coverage as in previous years.

KAMALA HARRIS CHOSEN AS VICE
PRESIDENTIAL CANDIDATE

Kamala Harris's name was one of the first to surface, and it seemed as though all other candidates that emerged were compared to her. Joe Biden chose Kamala Harris for many reasons: her proven national campaign experience, her tough rhetoric, and no doubt her diverse background as the daughter of a mother from India and a father from Jamaica. Harris had also been a close friend of Joe Biden's late son, Beau Biden. They had formed a friendship when both served as state attorney generals—Beau Biden for Delaware and Kamala Harris for California. The day after his Internet invitation to Harris to join him on the Democratic ticket, they appeared together to make their announcement at a high school gym in Delaware. In front of a backdrop of American flags, Joe Biden and Kamala Harris walked out with masks on. Biden began and called her a "fighter" and someone who "knows how to govern." He added, "She is ready on day one to lead." She is "well aware of the threats to this nation, and able to respond to them."[6]

As Kamala stepped up onto a platform in Wilmington, Delaware, she underscored Joe Biden's character and how she came to know about him through her friendship with his late son, Beau Biden. "Ever since I received the call, I've been thinking, yes, about the first Biden that I really came to know, and that of course is Joe's beloved son,"[7] the California senator said of Beau, who was forty-six when he died of brain cancer. "Let me just tell you about Beau Biden," Harris said, her voice filled with emotion. "I learned quickly that Beau was the kind of guy who inspired people to be a better version of themselves. He really was the best of us. And when I would ask him, 'Where'd you get that? Where'd this come from?' He'd always talk about his dad."[8]

Taking on the usual role of the vice president as a harsher critic of the opponent than the presidential candidate, Harris criticized Donald Trump's administration and vowed to hold him accountable for what is going on in the country, specifically his mishandling of the pandemic. She talked about her own personal story: about being a first generation American, about her past growing up. Starting with a litany of personal moments—loving to cook, being called "Momala," and so on—she transitioned into her personas as prosecutor and campaigner, It was easy to see a glimpse of a future president. She was part cheerleader for the campaign, part humble family woman, part fierce prosecutor and part skilled politician. She underscored her love for her family, her husband Doug and her step-children. With no audience (because of Covid-19), there was a certain intimacy to the campaign space, highlighting the warm relationship and personal connection that Biden and Harris share.

As the 2020 Democratic National Convention virtually kicked off, Kamala Harris began her remarks by recognizing the 100th anniversary of the passage of the 19th Amendment:

> Greetings America.
>
> It is truly an honor to be speaking with you.
>
> That I am here tonight is a testament to the dedication of generations before me. Women and men who believed so fiercely in the promise of equality, liberty, and justice for all.
>
> This week marks the one-hundredth anniversary of the passage of the 19th Amendment. And we celebrate the women who fought for that right.
>
> Yet so many of the Black women who helped secure that victory were still prohibited from voting, long after its ratification.
>
> But they were undeterred.
>
> Without fanfare or recognition, they organized, testified, rallied, marched, and fought—not just for their vote, but for a seat at the table. These women and the generations that followed worked to make democracy and opportunity real in the lives of all of us who followed.
>
> They paved the way for the trailblazing leadership of Barack Obama and Hillary Clinton.
>
> And these women inspired us to pick up the torch, and fight on.
>
> Women like Mary Church Terrell and Mary McCleod Bethune. Fannie Lou Hamer and Diane Nash. Constance Baker Motley and Shirley Chisholm.[9]

She spoke emotionally about a black man shot seven times in daylight in front of his children. "We must always defend peaceful protests and peaceful protesters," she said. "We should not confuse them with those looting and committing acts of violence, including the shooter who was arrested for murder. And make no mistake, we will not let these vigilantes and extremists derail the path to justice."

She also deeply criticized President Trump: "Donald Trump stood idly by and, folks, it was a deadly decision. Instead of rising to meet the most difficult moment of his presidency, Donald Trump froze." Earlier in her speech, Harris had characterized Trump as a failed president and asserted that the Republican National Convention was designed to soothe Trump's ego and make him feel good. "But here's the thing—he's the president of the United States," Harris continued. "And it's not supposed to be about him. It's supposed to be about the health, and the safety and the well-being of the American people."[10]

Harris also took the opportunity provided by Women's Equality Day to pen an op-ed in the *Washington Post* on the meaning of the 100th anniversary of ratification of the 19th Amendment. "Courageous American women had been organizing and protesting for seven decades to be treated as equal participants in our democracy, and their hard work finally paid off. After ratification votes from 36 states, it was official: Our Constitution would forevermore enshrine the right to vote for American women," she wrote. "That is, unless you were Black. Or Latina. Or Asian. Or Indigenous . . . . In fact, if I had been alive in 1920, I might not have been allowed to cast a ballot alongside White women. . . . It would be another forty-five years until the Voting Rights Act protected the voting rights of millions more voters of color."[11]

The attacks against Harris, that she is too weak on crime, or too tough on crime, that she is not a native-born American (similar to the birther questioning wielded against Barack Obama). None of them seemed to stick, but as the campaign went on, Harris had key moments to make her mark as the vice presidential candidate.

Because of Covid-19, the campaigning that Kamala Harris did was unlike any other VP candidate in modern history. She held "drive-in" rallies, where participants drove their cars into a large field to see her image on large screens and to listen from their car stereos. The indoor socially distanced rallies were marked by circles on the floor, six feet apart, amid mandatory mask wearing. When Election Day drew near, an unprecedented number of voters had already cast their ballots by mail, because for many the risk of going to a large, crowded voting precinct posed health risks. The night of the election, there was no clear winner, because it took election workers days to count the ballots in many states. By November 7, Joe Biden and Kamala Harris were declared the winners of the election, when the Commonwealth of Pennsylvania put their campaign beyond the 270 electoral votes needed to win.

OUR FIRST MADAM VICE PRESIDENT

Barbara Lee, a U.S. representative from California and former chair of the Congressional Black Caucus, has pointed out that six women, four of whom are sitting U.S. senators and two of whom are women of color, ran for president in 2020. For the first time in U.S. history, there was more than one woman candidate on the presidential debate stage—*that is progress.*[12] She further notes that "each of the women in the 2020 race broke barriers, challenged stereotypes, and helped us reimagine what a presidential candidate looks like."[13]

It seems fitting that at the one hundred-year mark of the women's right to vote, more women than ever ran for president. And yet, progress has been glacially slow. We want history to happen faster. However, like the builders of the world's greatest cathedrals, most of which took more than one hundred years to complete, we may not see this milestone reached in our lifetimes. It is true that many of the "cathedral builders" of women and the U.S. presidency—Margaret Chase Smith, Patsy Mink, Shirley Chisholm, and Geraldine Ferraro—did not live to see this shining moment.

The six women who vied for the presidency made a remarkable break with many women from the past who ran for high office: they reached that pinnacle with no (or few) familial ties. There was a time when the most likely way for a woman to enter U.S. politics was through familial ties: most notably, the death of her husband. This was especially true in Congress, and if it was not a husband who paved the way, it was a father who'd been successful in politics.

Margaret Chase Smith entered Congress as the result of her husband Clyde Smith's death. Clyde Smith, who was twenty-one years Margaret's senior, was a local politician. He mentored the teenage Margaret, offering her a job in his local political office—complete with courses in typing and shorthand. When he won a seat in the Maine legislature, he invited Margaret to work in his office. The two became an inseparable couple.

There is no doubt that her political star began to rise when she said "I do" and after ten years of marriage, she was known throughout the state as an astute politician in her own right. On his deathbed, Clyde Smith asked friends and supporters in the coming primary and general election to support his wife's candidacy. In fact, Margaret Chase Smith went on to have an especially fruitful political life and is far better remembered nationally than her late husband. She was a congresswoman, a senator, and a candidate for president. No one would deny that she was an able politician.

In 1999, Elizabeth Dole, the wife of former U.S. Senate majority leader and presidential nominee Bob Dole, made a nine-month exploratory bid for the U.S. presidency. As a young woman, growing up in the 1950s in North Carolina, she had dreamed of a life beyond Southern convention. After graduating from Duke University with a political science degree, she headed to Washington, DC, to consult with Margaret Chase Smith, then a U.S. senator from Maine (and the only woman senator). Chase Smith advised her that a law degree would be needed to navigate a life in politics in the nation's capital. Dole, after arming herself with a Harvard Law degree, worked for the Consumer Protection Bureau and met U.S. senator Robert Dole from Kansas. A few months into their marriage, Robert was selected as the vice presidential candidate, on the ticket with Gerald Ford, and Elizabeth was thrust into the national spotlight. Robert Dole would make a number of attempts at the presidency, finally winning the GOP nomination in 1996. When Elizabeth Dole made her speech at the convention, dozens of press and pundits asked why she wasn't the candidate. In 1999 she threw her hat in the ring, running against George W. Bush and Malcolm Stevenson "Steve" Forbes in the 2000 presidential election. But she dropped out in October 1999 because she did not have the financial wherewithal to compete with those who could practically self-fund their efforts.

Most famously of all, in 2008 and 2016 Hillary Clinton gained a place in history books as the first woman who won the Democratic nomination for president after having served as First Lady during the presidency of her husband, former two-term president Bill Clinton. This is not to say that Chase Smith, Dole and Clinton were not qualified to be president; however, in the minds of many Americans, they represented an extension of their husband's careers. We can never know for certain whether Margaret Chase, Elizabeth Hanford or Hillary Rodham would have become presidential candidates had they not been married to politicians. But we do know that they were first introduced to a national audience through their connection with their husbands. We can argue that Hillary Clinton, who as Wellesley valedictorian in 1969 was featured in *LIFE* magazine, and thus she drew national attention on her own. But it is still safe to say that her political career (fame and wealth—two presidential political requisites) took root as she served as First Lady to her husband, former president Bill Clinton.

In the Democratic primaries for president in 2020, however, none of the women had familial ties. None of these women entered politics on the coattails of their fathers or husbands. In this way, the 2020 election offered not only the most women in one presidential election, but a new era of women's presidential politics in the United States, one resulting purely from education, experience and personal ambition.

Carol Moseley Braun's entrance into the 2003 Democratic presidential primaries brought U.S. representative Shirley Chisholm's 1972 presidential run back into the spotlight. Numerous questions of interest immediately come to mind. Has the political environment for black females interested in the presidency changed? Is a black female candidate running nationally today in a better position than thirty years ago? Did black Americans see a black female as a serious contender in 2003 where they did not in 1972? Were blacks more inclined to support a black male in the race—such as the Reverend Al Sharpton—regardless of the qualifications of Moseley Braun? While data are limited, this article attempts to address these questions and to draw some conclusions. Kamala Harris's bid for president also brought Shirley Chisholm's presidential bid back into focus, perhaps suggesting that Harris faced the same kinds of obstacles encountered by Moseley Braun, first encountered by Chisholm—the double bias of race and gender.

In any event, in the context of the changing demographics of the United States, Joe Biden's selection of Kamala Harris "has been celebrated as a milestone because she is the first black woman and the first of Indian descent in American history to be on a major party's presidential ticket. But her selection also highlights a remarkable shift in this country: the rise of a new wave of children of immigrants, or second-generation Americans, as a growing political and cultural force, different from any that has come before."[14] Another observer noted, "The Democratic ticket was an unlikely partnership: forged in conflict and fused over Zoom, divided by generation, race and gender. They come from different coasts, differed ideologies, different Americas."[15] Because of these stark differences, the election of Kamala Harris as vice president changes the rhetoric of women and presidential politics not only because it is a first—but because it puts a woman into the highest place of power in the United States. No longer merely a fictional character on television or the movies, when any-one in the United States or around the world consumes politics from the United States, a woman, Vice President Harris will be a key player. Joe Biden knows firsthand the important way a president can boost the experience and visibility of the vice president. He is committed to have Harris serve in the same way he served President Obama. "He has made the same committed he extracted from Barack Obama: that the VP will be the last person in the room after meetings, consulted on all big decisions. The two communicate every day.[16]

Just as the election of Barack Obama as the first African American presi-dent did not end racial injustice in our country, the election of Kamala Harris as vice president will not end gender inequality. When we look to the future of women and presidential politics, we can identify a number of women already in political life who could become contenders.

Who are the women in the pipeline for presidential politics in the future? It can be anyone's guess, since politics and politicians rise and fall swiftly. It used to be that governors were the key to the presidency, but after the United States elected Barack Obama, that became less true. And yet, for women, who often need more credentials, not less, it may still hold true that the path to the presidency for a woman may be a governorship. (That is, holding the top elected executive-branch office in the state may be seen as better preparation for the Oval Office, especially during a critical time like the Covid-19 pan-demic, when governors began to play a more prominent role in the nation's everyday political media landscape.) Of course, none of the women who ran for the Democratic primary were governors, and each woman profiled in this book was at the top of the list of presidential possibilities for the future. In addition to the six profiled in the book, here are brief profiles of women to keep an eye on. They are on the list because they are either currently governors, or they have been mentioned as presidential or vice presidential possibilities.

THE GOVERNORS

Gretchen Whitmer is a Democrat who serves as the forty-ninth governor of Michigan. Previously she served in the Michigan House of Representatives from 2001 to 2006 and in the Michigan Senate from 2006 to 2015. Mentioned repeatedly as a short-list vice presidential possibility for Joe Biden, she drew national attention during the Covid-19 crisis and was dubbed "that woman" by President Trump, who derided her for requesting much-needed supplies for her state to complete medical testing and to protect front-line medical workers.

Gina Raimondo is the seventy-fifth governor of Rhode Island. A Democrat, she served previously as the general treasurer of the state. She came to national attention during the Covid-19 crisis for her daily briefings to her state constituents. She was mentioned by *The New York Times* as a possible vice presidential contender.[17]

Katherine "Kate" Brown, a Democrat, serves as the thirty-eighth governor of Oregon. She was a congresswoman from 1991 to 1997, and Oregon state senator (Twenty-First District) from 1997 to 2009. She served three terms as majority leader of the Oregon state senate and two terms as Oregon's secretary of state.

Kay Ellen Ivey has served as the fifty-fourth governor of Alabama since 2017. A member of the Republican Party, she was the thirty-eighth Alabama state treasurer from 2003 to 2011 and the thirtieth lieutenant governor of Alabama from 2011 to 2017.

Kimberly Kay Reynolds, a Republican, is the forty-third governor of Iowa. She previously served as the lieutenant governor, and before that she was the Clarke County treasurer. She also served four terms in the Iowa Senate.

Michelle Grisham is a Democrat serving as the thirty-second governor of New Mexico. Previously she served in Congress from 2013 to 2018. She was mentioned by the *New York Times* as a possible presidential contender.[18]

Janet Mills is a Democrat who serves as the seventy-fifth governor of Maine. She previously served as the Maine attorney general.

Kristi Noem is a Republican and the thirty-third governor of South Dakota. She was a congresswoman from 2011 to 2019 and a state senator from 2007 to 2011.

Laura Kelly is a Democrat and the forty-eighth governor of Kansas. She represented the Eighteenth District in the Kansas Senate from 2005 to 2009.

Former South Carolina governor Nikki Haley is a Republican, a former South Carolina state legislator, and a former U.S. ambassador to the United Nations.

Other notables:

Stacey Abrams is a Democrat who served in the Georgia House of Representative from 2007 to 2017 and as its minority leader from 2011 to 2017. In 2018 she was a gubernatorial candidate who lost to Brian Kemp, without conceding the election, because it was so close. Her race drew national attention because she was the first African American female candidate in Georgia; in 2019 she delivered the response to the State of the Union address. Her star will likely rise, since she is credited with campaigning heavily for Joe Biden and Kamala Harris in Georgia.

Alexandria Ocasio-Cortez is an American politician serving as the U.S. representative for New York's Fourteenth District. The district includes the eastern part of the Bronx and portions of north-central Queens in New York City. A member of the Democratic Party, she has a national reputation for her far-left leanings and for support of the Green New Deal and for Bernie Sanders's presidential campaign.

Dynastic possibilities include Chelsea Clinton, the daughter of former president Bill Clinton and former First Lady Hillary Clinton, who also served as U.S. senator from New York, U.S. secretary of state, and Democratic presidential nominee. HiDaughters of President Donald Trump, Ivanka Trump or Tiffany Trump, could potentially reemerge on the political scene, having gained national recognition during their father's presidential service.

When Senator Elizabeth Warren's ran for president, she often gave a "pinky promise" to the little girls who came to meet her, and when she did that she tried to show little girls that running for president is "what girls do." We know from our research that voters' unconscious bias remains a very real obstacle, especially when it comes to women running for executive office. While we may not get to see a woman in the Oval Office in 2020, we can help women who run in the future by challenging that bias each and every day.

As the Covid-19 pandemic spread across the globe, it was noted repeatedly in the press that the countries with women leaders universally had fewer deaths and more testing than countries with male leaders. As *ForbesWomen* contributor Marianne Schnall noted in a profile of ten women leaders, "the efficacy of female leaders handling this pandemic, and what we can learn from what leadership qualities and skills women bring to leadership, are lessons worth noting as we seek to rebuild our country, economy, and address the many problems we face as a nation and world."[19] These lessons are certainly worth noting as we move toward electing a woman as U.S. president. By the time the United States had its first woman nominee for president in 2016, dozens of other countries, including India, Croatia and Slovenia, had already elected women as heads of state.

This analysis is presented humbly because, when it comes to women and presidential leadership, we have a very small "n"—that is, a very small sample size—and we are learning as we are going along. Will the six women who ran for president in 2020 engender more women running for president in every election in the future? My hypothesis is yes. At this critical time in history, it's worth recognizing that the tropes women have to confront that men don't—that they are too mean, too old, too blonde, too "woo-woo," or too angry to be elected president—are just that: sexist tropes. Regardless, the six women who ran for president in 2020 have been catalysts for progress for gender parity in the U.S. presidency. We already see a rapid acceleration in the numbers of women running for political office; that we have a woman vice president, who is consistently being thought of and written about as presidential, represents tremendous progress.

While campaigning for president, Kamala Harris repeatedly said that she had "faith in the American people to know that we will never be burdened by the assumptions of who can do what, based on who historically has done it."[20] In her acceptance of the nomination, Harris underscored that the work of gender equality in the United States is far from over and credited Joe Biden for having the audacity "to break one of the most substantial barriers that exists in our country" and choose a woman as his vice president. "But while I may be the first woman in this office, I won't be the last. Because every little girl watching tonight sees that this is a country of possibilities."[21] The visual of Kamala Harris as vice president from her February 2021 cover of *Vogue* donning her trademark "Chucks" sneakers, to the multitude of meetings and press events to follow, Harris will change what people think of when they conjure up an image of what a U.S. vice president looks like.

Tulsi Gabbard, the young Hawaiian congresswoman and military veteran who urged peace. Kirsten Gillibrand, who made her announcement in front of Trump Tower and called out greed and corruption while underscoring the need to believe women. Amy Klobuchar, the whip-smart, winning U.S. senator from Minnesota. Kamala Harris, who participated in civil rights marches from her stroller, Elizabeth Warren, who argued that if we can get the economy right, then the nation will be better. Marianne Williamson, who offered a history lesson wrapped up in love. These are the women who made a strong collective impact on women and the American presidency, all in one election.

Kamala Harris, after accepting her nomination for vice president, was joined by her jubilant family on stage to celebrate the milestone event. Grinning and embracing her were her husband, Doug Emhoff, her step-children Cole and Ella, her sister Mia and her niece, entrepreneur Meena Harris. With Meena were her two daughters, about the same ages of the two little girls in the row in front of mine in Philadelphia at the Democratic National Convention four years earlier. Both evenings, no doubt, made lasting impressions on those two sets of young girls—as the groundbreaking events of those evenings must have done for the entire nation. Progress has been slow for women and political parity in the United States, but it has been progress nonetheless—because women have persisted. It signals to girls that a path is open to them that previously was not. The election of Kamala Harris as vice president changes a long-held social fact in the United States that men ascend to the presidency and vice-presidency and women do not. The catalyst for this change has been inching forward for decades, but was given a firm shove in the 2020 primary for president when six women—Tulsi Gabbard, Kirsten Gillibrand, Amy Klobuchar, Kamala Harris, Elizabeth Warren, and Marianne Williamson—the largest number of women running for president at one time mounted their campaigns for the presidency. It reminds us that progress can be slow, but for all the ills of 2020, this leap forward cannot be denied. Because, when women run, we all win.

NOTES

1. Kathleen Dolan, *When Does Gender Matter? Women Candidates & Gender Stereotypes in American Elections* (New York, NY: Oxford University Press, 2014).

2. https://www.nbcnews.com/politics/2020-election/black-woman-not-must-biden-s-running-mate-clyburn-says-n1194926.

3. Mark Leibovich, "The End of 'Who Me? For V.P.?' Politics," *The New York Times*, May 19, 2020, https://www.nytimes.com/2020/05/19/us/politics/biden-vice-president-trump.html?action=click&module=q1qUTop%20Stories&pgtype=Homepage (accessed May 19, 2020).

4. Alexander Burns, "Joe Biden's Vice-Presidential Pick: Kamala Harris," *The New York Times*, June 22, 2020, https://www.nytimes.com/article/biden-vice-president-2020.html (accessed June 23, 2020).

5. Cami Anderson, "Here's Why That Letter From Women Leaders To The News Media Is Such a Big Deal," *Forbes*, August 11, 2020, https://www.forbes.com/sites/camianderson1/2020/08/11/heres-why-that-letter-from-women-leaders-to-the-news-media-is-such-a-bfd/#600c0cec493f (accessed August 17, 2020).

6. Karl Baker and Meredith Neuman, "Kamala Harris embraces VP bid in Delaware with speech that scorches Trump's record," *Delaware News Journal*, August 12, 2020, https://www.delawareonline.com/story/news/2020/08/12/kamala-harris-embraces-vp-role-delaware-speech-scorches-trumps-record/3353025001/ (accessed November 8, 2020).

7. Transcript: "Kamala Harris kicks off presidential campaign in Oakland," KTVU Fox 2, January 27, 2019, https://www.ktvu.com/news/transcript-kamala-harris-kicks-off-presidential-campaign-in-oakland (accessed August 13, 2020).

8. Ibid.

9. NBC News, "Watch Kamala Harris' Full Remarks At The 2020 DNC," posted to YouTube August 19, 2020, https://www.youtube.com/watch?v=_Vyqn-7ibeM (accessed August 27, 2020).

10. Kamala Harris, Speech Transcript August 27: COVID-19 & Economy, posted to Rev Transcripts on August 27, 2020, https://www.rev.com/blog/transcripts/kamala-harris-speech-transcript-august-27-covid-19-economy (accessed August 28, 2020).

11. Kamala D. Harris, "Kamala Harris: Voting is the best way to honor generations of women who paved the way for me," *The Washington Post*, August 26, 2020, https://www.washingtonpost.com/opinions/kamala-harris-womens-equality

-day-19th-amendment/2020/08/25/7c268a82-e704-11ea-97e0-94d2e46e759b_story
.html(accessed August 27, 2020).

12. Barbara Lee Family Foundation, letter to followers via email, March 20, 2020.

13. Ibid.

14. Sabrina Tavernise, "Kamala Harris, Daughter of Immigrants, Is the Face of America's Changing Demographic Shift," *The New York Times*, August 16, 2020, A1.

15. Alter, Charlotte, "Joe Biden and Kamala Harris, President-Elect and Vice-President Elect of the United States, TIME, December 21/288, 2020, 46.

16. Ibid.

17. Burns, "Joe Biden's VP Pick."

18. Ibid.

19. Marianne Schnall, "Ten Prominent Women Spotlight The Need For Women's Leadership During The Pandemic And Beyond," *Forbes*, May 15, 2020. https://www
.forbes.com/sites/marianneschnall/2020/05/18/ten-prominent-women-spotlight-need
-forwomens-leadershipduring-pandemic/#5741f7082498 (accessed May 18, 2020).

20. Kelly Dittmar and Glynda Carr, "Kamala Harris' Liability Was Not Electability," *Ms.*, December 19, 2019, https://msmagazine.com/2019/12/19/kamala
-harris-liability-was-not-electability/ (accessed August 13, 2020).

21. Matt Stevens, "Read Kamala Harris's Vice President-Elect Acceptance Speech," *The New York Times*, November 8, 2020, https://www.nytimes.com/article/
watch-kamala-harris-speech-video-transcript.html (accessed November 6, 2020).

Afterword

by Congresswoman Susan Wild

"When women run, women win." Nothing proved that premise more than the midterm elections of 2018, when I (and 35 other women running for Congress) won our Democratic primaries and then went on to win in the general election held on November 8, 2018. In addition, one Republican woman was newly elected. In January of 2019, these first-time members became part of a record-setting ninety Democratic women (and fifteen Republican women) to be sworn in to Congress, making the 116th Congress the most estrogen-intensive of any new Congress.

However, even with that major accomplishment, Congress remained overwhelmingly male. Just 23.4 percent of the 435 members of the House of Representatives were female. But, the increase from the 115th Congress was noticeable—and noted—by many in the political world. Republicans, who had had a very poor showing in the 2018 midterms, immediately embarked on a plan to recruit, train, and elect more women to their caucus. As of the time of this writing, twenty-six Republican women were elected in November 2020, showing that their party's plan had worked. Yet, a number of the Democratic women who had first been elected in 2018 lost their seats in 2020, most often to a Republican woman. The total balance between men and women in the 117th Congress will be approximately one percent to four percent respectively.[1]

Clearly, we can accept without hesitation the premise that "when women run, women win." And, given the marked differences between the platforms of Democrats and Republicans running for Congress in 2020, it is fair to say that gender played a greater role than did the policy positions of the candidates. Many of the 2020 contests were between two women (my own included). Yet to think that there were similarities between the opposing candidates—other than the obvious—would be to overstate the proposition that women are more appealing candidates to voters in today's times than are men. Quite simply, the positions of a candidate were far easier to generalize based on her political affiliation than her gender. Republican women embraced Republican talking points and positions. Democratic women generally did the same with Democratic messaging and policies. However, perhaps for the first time ever, in 2018 and again in 2020, simply being a qualified woman (rather than a man) seemed to confer an advantage to the female candidate, regardless of which political party the candidate claimed as her own. Fundraising (a key marker of success) among female candidates of both political parties was robust, and often exceeded similarly situated male candidates.

I suspect that we will continue to see the number of women running for office increase every year, and it would not surprise me at all if we have more women running than men within a decade, much as there are now more women law graduates than men, whereas when I graduated in 1982, approximately 30 percent of my class was female. That alone is progress, of course. But, until we see the success of women who are not judged differently than their male counterparts, we will still have a lot of work to do.

Looking around the floor of the House of Representatives, I see men who are fat, thin, tall, short, conventionally attractive, and some who would be considered ugly. The vast majority are white. Almost all of them wear the same uniform of a dark suit and tie, and could easily get away with the same basic attire every day. Every single one of them were elected in their own right, without much discussion of their physical attributes. An attractive wife and well-mannered children are a plus for them in their campaigns.

The women are almost uniformly well-groomed, sometimes excessively so. Their wardrobes are colorful, varied, and often punishing (specifically, the stiletto heels worn by Speaker of the House Nancy Pelosi are brutal on the feet when one walks the long marble hallways. Yet, a number of women wear those heels, although many others have opted for practical and foot-saving flats.) Fewer women who currently serve would ever be characterized as frumpy than one has fingers on a hand. Physical appearance is still an extremely important factor in the success of women in politics, just as in the boardroom. A female candidate is very likely to be asked about her family and children, and who will be caring for them while she is in Congress.

But what I have found encouraging is the amount of airtime and newsprint devoted to covering the actual words that are coming out of those women's mouths. There are no shrinking violets in the group. Some of the women in the 116th Congress are household names across the country—Alexandria Ocasio-Cortez, Katie Porter, Cheri Bustos, Abigail Spanberger, and, of course, the speaker herself. The chair of the powerful House Committee on Appropriations will pass from Nita Lowey (the first chairwoman, elected to that position in the 116th Congress) to Rosa DeLauro, who will serve as such in the 117th. (Indeed, all three of the contenders for that powerful Chair position were female—DeLauro, Debbie Wasserman-Schultz, and Marcy Kaptur.) The next assistant speaker of the House will be Katherine Clark. The chairwoman of the Committee on Oversight is Carolyn Maloney. And I could go on.

Just as there are now more female lawyers and doctors than this country has ever seen before, the time will come (soon) when being a female politician will not be remarkable. And perhaps the best thing about that will be that these women will be evaluated by voters for the work they do, rather than the clothes they wear.

The hard work that has been done by so many to advance the cause of women in the political system cannot be underestimated. When I first considered running for Congress, I first questioned my own credentials, and worried that I would not be able to find a base of support, or worse, that I wouldn't be up for the challenges of the job (despite a thirty-plus-year career as a courtroom lawyer, trying many complicated cases every year). A fortuitous phone call from EMILY's List gave me just the amount of confidence I needed to forge ahead. I was assured that they would help me create the infrastructure I needed for a campaign, although it would be up to me to raise the money needed to launch and to get through a six-way primary against five male opponents. I was told bluntly that it would be harder for me to raise money than it would be for the men, and this turned out to be true. But simply knowing that there was an organization of committed people devoted to helping women win elected office made all the difference in the world. The point is that EMILY's List extended a hand to me, as did many other organizations and people in the months after. The time will come when women don't need that hand—in fact, for many younger women now, that time is already here. But for me, it meant the world.

Most rewarding in my first campaign, by far, was the excitement I could see and hear from lots of "ordinary" women whom I came to know over the course of my year-and-a-half candidacy. From older women came comments about feeling that they had had to wait far too long to be represented by a woman—often with laments about the disappointing loss of Hillary Clinton in 2016. From younger women came excitement about the fact that "someone who could be their mom" was running for federal office. From young girls, of all races and ethnicities, I heard exclamations about their own political ambitions—most notably from a young Muslim girl in a headscarf who enthusiastically and publicly shared with me her ambition to be president of the United States. And from a large number of men, I heard the refrain "it's time to let women run the country; the men have messed it all up."

In the two-plus years I have served in Congress, I have come to learn this: running for office is hard; in fact, it is grueling. The work itself is rewarding but frustrating, energizing but exhausting. In that, it is not much different than the work that women have done for centuries. We can do this. And it's worth it.

NOTE

1. One seat in NY-22 remains to be determined as of this writing, which will either be won by a Democratic man or a Republican woman.

Selected Bibliography

Allen, Terina, "'Are You Mocking Me?' Amy Klobuchar Isn't Just Fighting For The Nomination—She's Fighting For Her Career," *Forbes*, February 20, 2020, https://www.forbes.com/sites/terinaallen/2020/02/20/are-you-mocking-me-why-it-boiled-over-between-amy-klobuchar-and-pete-buttigieg/#2b04703e4b94 (accessed September 10, 2020).

Angell, Tom, "Tulsi Gabbard Endorses Legalizing Drugs," *Forbes.com*, January 19, 2020. https://www.forbes.com/sites/tomangell/2020/01/19/tulsi-gabbard-endorses-legalizing-drugs/#776ea3396ed4 (accessed March 25, 2020).

Astor, Maggie, "Amy Klobuchar Compares Pete Buttigieg to Trump," *The New York Times*, February 8, 2020. (accessed February 8, 2020).

Baker, Karl and Meredith Neuman, "Kamala Harris embraces VP bid in Delaware with speech that scorches Trump's record," *Delaware News Journal*, August 12, 2020, https://www.delawareonline.com/story/news/2020/08/12/kamala-harris-embraces-vp-role-delaware-speech-scorches-trumps-record/3353025001/ (accessed November 8, 2020).

Baker, Peter, "On Day 1,001, Trump Made It Clear: Being 'Presidential' Is Boring," *The New York Times*, October 18, 2019. https://www.nytimes.com/2019/10/18/us/politics/trump-presidency.html (accessed May 28, 2020).

Ball, Molly, "Finding Kamala Harris: Emphatic But Elusive, the Candidate Searches for her Place in the Democratic Field," TIME, October 14, 2019, 33.

Ball, Molly, "The Strife of the Party: The Democrats' debate will shape America's Future," TIME, August 5, 2020, 21.

Beene, Ryan, Bill Allison and Hailey Waller, "Klobuchar's Rise Brings New Scrutiny to Record as Prosecutor, February 16, 2020, https://www.bloomberg.com/news/articles/2020-02-16/klobuchar-says-she-s-raised-12-million-online-since-n-h-debate (accessed February 19, 2020).

Beggin, Riley, "Tulsi Gabbard calls Hillary Clinton "the queen of warmongers" in her latest clash with top Democrats," *Vox*, October 19, 2019, https://www.vox.com

/policy-and-politics/2019/10/19/20922122/hillary-clinton-tulsi-gabbard-queen
-warmongers-russia-2020-election (accessed October 21, 2019).

Bower, C. L. "Public discourse and female presidential candidates," in *Anticipating Madam President*, eds. R. P. Watson and A. Gordon (Boulder, CO: Lynne Rienner Publishers, Inc., 2003), 107–116.

Bowles, Nellie, "Gabbard, a Soldier Who Is Serious About Peace," The New York Times, August 3, 2019, A-1.

Bromwich, Jonah Engel, "I Quit the Presidential Campaign," *The New York Times*, January 20, 2020, https://www.nytimes.com/2020/01/20/style/marianne-william-son-presidential-race.html (accessed February 15, 2020).

Bufkin, Ellie, "'That little girl was me': Kamala Harris says she was a victim of Biden's anti-busing racial policies," *The Washington Examiner*, June 27, 2019, https://www.washingtonexaminer.com/news/kamala-harris-says-she-was-a-victim -of-bidens-racial-policies (accessed August 17, 2020).

Burns, Alexander, "Joe Biden's Vice-Presidential Pick: Kamala Harris," *The New York Times*, June 22, 2020, https://www.nytimes.com/article/biden-vice-president -2020.html (accessed June 23, 2020).

Burns, Alexander, "Gillibrand Drops Out of 2020 Presidential Race," *The New York Times*, August 28, 2019, https://www.nytimes.com/2019/08/28/us/politics/kirsten -gillibrand-2020-drop-out.html (accessed January 13, 2020).

Caldego, Christopher, "How Harris Went from 'Female Obama' to Fifth Place," *Politico*, November 5, 2019, https://www.politico.com/magazine/story/2019/11 /05/how-kamala-harris-went-from-female-obama-to-fifth-place-229901 (accessed March 29, 2020).

Clift, Eleanor and Tom Brazaitis, *Madame President: Shattering the Last Glass Ceiling* (New York: Scribner, 2000).

Concha, Joe, "Gabbard Says She Received No Reason," *The Hill,* January 29, 2020. https://thehill.com/homenews/campaign/480441-gabbard-says-shes-received-no -reason-from-cnn-for-non-invitation-to-town (accessed January 30, 2020).

Corsaniti, Nick, "Marianne Williamson on Race, Reparations and Trump's 'Dark Psychic Force,' " *The New York Times,* July 31, 2019, https://www.nytimes.com /2019/07/30/us/politics/marianne-williamson-debate-quotes.html (accessed July 31, 2019).

Corasanti, Nick and Katie Glueck, "Protests in Minnesota Renew Scrutiny of Klobuchar's Record as Prosecutor," *The New York Times*, May 28, 2020, https:// www.nytimes.com/2020/05/29/us/politics/klobuchar-minneapolis-george-floyd .html (accessed May 28, 2020).

Dolan, Kathleen, *When Does Gender Matter? Women Candidates & Gender Stereotypes in American Elections* (New York, NY: Oxford University Press, 2014).

Entman, Liz, "Grassley, Klobuchar Most Effective Senators of 115th Congress According to Study," Vanderbilt University, February 28, 2019, https://news .vanderbilt.edu/2019/02/28/grassley-klobuchar-most-effective-senators-of-115th -congress-according-to-study/ (accessed February 12, 2020).

Epstein, Alan, "Amy Klobuchar fans braved a blizzard to watch her 2020 US presi-dential bid announcement," *Quartz*, February 10, 2019. https://qz.com/1547041

/amy-klobuchar-fans-braved-a-blizzard-to-watch-her-2020-us-presidential-bid -announcement/ (accessed October 11, 2019).

Epstein, Reid J. "Candidates Are Pushed to Go Viral, or Risk Being Left Behind," *The New York Times*, July 20, 2019, A20.

Falk, Erica and Kathleen Hall Jamieson, "Changing the Climate of Expectations," in *Anticipating Madam President*, eds. Robert P. Watson and Ann Gordon (Boulder, CO: Lynne Rienner Publishers, 2003), 49.

Feinberg, Ashley, "Bloomberg on Being Accused of Sexual Harassment: They Didn't Like a Joke I Told," *Slate*, February 19, 2020, https://slate.com/news-and-politics /2020/02/bloomberg-on-being-accused-of-sexual-harassment-the-didnt-like-a-joke -i-told.html (accessed June 9, 2020).

Flanagan, Kate, "The Anger of Amy Klobuchar," *The Atlantic*, March 5, 2019. https:// www.theatlantic.com/ideas/archive/2019/03/telling-reactions-tales-amy-klobu- chars-rage/584104/ (accessed May 27, 2020).

Flegenheimer, Matt and Sydney Ember, "How Amy Klobuchar Treats Her Staff," *The New York Times*, February 22, 2019, A-1.

Forgey, Quint, "Tulsi Gabbard Says She Won't Run for Re-Election, " Politico, October 25, 2019, https://www.politico.com/news/2019/10/25/tulsi-gabbard-wont -run-congress-reelection-2020-057222 (accessed October 26, 2019).

Fox, Richard L. 2011. "Studying Gender in U.S. Politics: Where Do We Go from Here?", *Politics & Gender* 7(1): 94–99.

Gillibrand, Kirsten, Off the Sidelines, New York: Ballantine Books, 2014.

Goldberg, Jonah Goldberg, "Biden Facing a Marketing Decision on His Running Mate," *The Morning Call* (Allentown, PA) May 28, 2020, 17.

Goldmacher, Shane, "She Has A Plan For Telephoning Early and Often," *The New York Times*, December 28, 2019. A-1.

Goldmacher, Shane, "In Iowa, a Bid to Make Up for Lost Time," *The New York Times*, August 12, 2019, A10.

Goldmacher, Shane and Astead W. Herndon, "Warren's Plan for Bankruptcy Law Recalls Clash in Senate with Biden," *The New York Times*, January 8, 2020, A14.

Goodyear, Dana, "Kamala Harris Makes Her Case," *The New Yorker*, July 15, 2019, https://www.newyorker.com/magazine/2019/07/22/kamala-harris-makes-her-case (accessed April 2, 2020).

Harris, Kamala D. "Kamala Harris: Voting is the best way to honor generations of women who paved the way for me," *The Washington Post*, August 26, 2020, https:// www.washingtonpost.com/opinions/kamala-harris-womens-equality-day-19th -amendment/2020/08/25/7c268a82-e704-11ea-97e0-94d2e46e759b_story.html.

Harris, Kamala, *The Truths We Hold: An American Journey*, New York: Penguin, 2019.

Healy, Patrick and Amy Chozick, "Hillary Clinton Warns of 'Moment of Reckoning' in Speech Accepting Nomination," *The New York Times*, July 28, 2016, https:// www.nytimes.com/2016/07/29/us/politics/dnc-hillary-clinton-speech.html?sea rchResultPosition=6 (accessed March 6, 2020).

Herndon, Astead W., "Harris says 'Trust Me' On Need for Criminal Justice Reform," *The New York Times*, September 10, 2019, A16.

Herndon, Astead W. "Why Kamala Harris Is Not Clamoring To Be Joe Biden's Running Mate," *The New York Times*, May 11, 2020, https://www.nytimes.com/2020/05/11/us/politics/kamala-harris-biden-vp.html?searchResultPosition=1 (accessed May 15, 2020).

Honan, Edith, "'That little girl was me,': Kamala Harris and Biden Spar Over Desegregation at Debate," *ABC News*, June 27, 2019, https://abcnews.go.com/Politics/girl-senator-harris-vice-president-biden-spar-desegregation/story?id=64007842 (accessed February 1, 2021).

Jacobs, Emily, "Bloomberg claimed he 'didn't realize' Warren was still running," *New York Post*, March 3, 2020. https://nypost.com/2020/03/03/bloomberg-claimed-he-didnt-realize-warren-was-still-running/ (accessed March 3, 2020).

Jaffe, Alexandra, "Buttigieg, Sanders campaigns request Iowa caucus recanvass." Arizona Republican, February 3, 2020, A-1.

Jones, Lloyd, "Tulsi Gabbard Parries Sun's Questions And Then Heads for the Slopes," The Sun, January 28, 2020,https://www.conwaydailysun.com/news/local/gabbard-parries-sun-s-questions-then-hits-the-slopes/article_cef72df0-4206-11ea-93e6-db5d211fe641.html (accessed January 30, 2020).

Kantor, Jodi and Megan Twohey, *She Said: Breaking the Sexual Harassment Story That Helped Ignite A Movement*. New York: Penguin Press, 2019, 186.

Kaplan, Thomas, "Warren's Slam on Delaney Was Called the Line of the Night. Here's What She Said," *The New York Times*, July 31, 2019, https://www.nytimes.com/2019/07/30/us/politics/elizabeth-warren-debate.html (accessed July 31, 2019).

Kilgore, Ed, "Looks Like the 2020 Democratic Presidential Field Could Be the Largest Ever," *New York*, February 13, 2019, https://nymag.com/intelligencer/2019/02/2020-democratic-presidential-field-could-be-the-largest-ever.html (accessed March 23, 2020).

"Kirsten Gillibrand's Clorox Comment the Debate Moment of the Night," Marie Claire, August 1, 2019 https://www.marieclaire.com/culture/a28571332/kirsten-gillibrand-clorox-debate/ (accessed January 13, 2020).

Klobuchar, Amy, "Amy Klobuchar: The Right Way to Vote This November," *The New York Times*, April 14, 2020, https://www.nytimes.com/2020/04/14/opinion/klobuchar-coronavirus-mail-voting.html (accessed May 27, 2020).

Klobuchar, Amy, *The Senator Next Door* (New York: Henry Holt, 2015).

Kurtzelblen, Danielle, "Fact Check: Gillibrand Attacks Biden on 'deterioration of the family' Op/Ed, August 1, 2019, https://www.npr.org/2019/08/01/747122903/fact-check-gillibrand-attacks-biden-on-1981-deterioration-of-family-op-ed (accessed January 13, 2020).

Leibovich, Mark, "The End of 'Who Me? For V.P.?' Politics," *The New York Times*, May 19, 2020, https://www.nytimes.com/2020/05/19/us/politics/biden-vice-president-trump.html?action=click&module=q1qUTop%20Stories&pgtype=Homepage (accessed May 19, 2020).

Lerer, Lisa, "Amy Klobuchar: The senator from Minnesota wants to lower drug prices and bridge the rural-urban divide," *The New York Times*, January 31, 2020, "https://www.nytimes.com/interactive/2020/01/31/us/politics/amy-klobuchar-campaign-speech.html," (accessed September 2, 2020).

Lerer, Lisa and Jennifer Medina, "The Burdens of Black Women in Politics," *The New York Times*, December 9, 2019, A11.

Lerer, Lisa and Maggie Astor, "Gabbard Drops Out of Presidential Race," The New York Times, March 19, 2020. https://www.nytimes.com/2020/03/19/us/politics/tulsi-gabbard-drops-out.html?action=click&module=Latest&pgtype=Homepage (accessed March 20, 2020).

Li, David K. "Lock Her Up Chant Breaks Out While Trump Speaks to Veterans Group," *New York Post*, July 26, 2016, https://nypost.com/2016/07/26/lock-her-up-chant-breaks-out-while-trump-speaks-to-veterans-group/ (accessed October 23, 2020).

Marks, Peter, "Elizabethan: Warren knows the power of words," *The Washington Post*, August 21, 2019, https://www.washingtonpost.com/arts-entertainment/2019/08/21/posts-theater-critic-is-reviewing-performances-democratic-candidates-this-installment-elizabeth-warren-cuts-shakespearean-figure-arizona/?arc404=true (accessed September 23, 2020).

Martin, Douglas, "She Ended the Men's Club in National Politics," *The New York Times*, March 26, 2011, https://www.nytimes.com/2011/03/27/us/politics/27geraldine-ferraro.html (accessed March 27, 2020).

Medina, Jennifer, "A Little Bit Stand-Up, and a Little Bit Stump Speech," *The New York Times*, November 7, 2019. A10.

Medina, Jennifer, "They Saw Themselves in Elizabeth Warren. So What Do They See Now?" *The New York Times*, https://www.nytimes.com/2020/02/28/us/politics/elizabeth-warren-women-voters.html?action=click&module=Top%20Stories&pgtype=Homepage (accessed February 27, 2020).

Mehta, Seema, Michael Finnegan and Melanie Mason, "Elizabeth Warren says Bernie Sanders told her a woman couldn't win the presidency," *Los Angeles Times*, https://www.latimes.com/politics/story/2020-01-13/benie-sanders-elizabeth-warren-campaigns-on-the-attack (accessed January 14, 2020).

Montifore, Simon Sebag, "Marianne Williamson: Who Is She & Why Do We Need Her Now?", Psychology Today, July 1, 1992, 22.

Mullany, Gerry, "Gabbard Won't Seek Fifth Term in Congress: Possible Third Party Bid for Presidency," *The New York Times*, October 26, 2019, A11.

Neal, Spencer, "There Are Consequences To Elections," February 10, 2020, Washington Examiner, https://www.washingtonexaminer.com/news/there-are-consequences-to-elections-tulsi-gabbard-defends-trump-firing-of-vindman (accessed February 2, 2021).

Norander, Stephanie Norander, (2017), "Kamala Harris and the interruptions heard around the internet," *Feminist Media Studies*, 17:6, 1104–1107, DOI: 10.1080/14680777.2017.1380427.

Pearce, Tim, "Hillary Clinton Says Tulsi Gabbard is a Russian Asset," The Washington Examiner, October 18, 2019, https://www.washingtonexaminer.com/news/hillary-clinton-says-tulsi-gabbard-is-a-russian-asset-groomed-to-ensure-trump-re-election (accessed October 18, 2019).

Peoples, Steve, Meg Kinnard and Bill Barrow, "Dem Candidates Attach Bloomberg, Sanders in Debate," *The Arizona Republic*, February 26, 2020, A-1.

Powers, John. "Tulsi Gabbard is Making a Splash," *Vogue*, June 24, 2013 https://www.vogue.com/article/making-a-splash-is-tulsi-gabbard-the-next-democratic-party-star (accessed October 21, 2019).

Quinn, Sally, "A Conversation with Marianne Williamson," *The Washington Post / LIVE*, October 1, 2020 https://www.washingtonpost.com/video/washington-post-live/a-conversation-with-marianne-williamson/2020/10/01/9321d868-8db7-4a23-8732-469db5144619_video.html (accessed October 2, 2020).

Rozsa, Matthew, "Tulsi Gabbard says Democratic Rival Kamala Harris 'Is Not Qualified to Serve as Commander-in-Chief,' " *Salon*, July 24, 2019. https://www.salon.com/2019/07/24/tulsi-gabbard-says-democratic-rival-kamala-harris-is-not-qualified-to-serve-as-commander-in-chief/ (accessed March 25, 2020).

Rozsa, Matthew, Tulsi Gabbard: Impeachment "Increased the Likelihood that Donald Trump Will Remain the President," Salon, December 31, 2019. https://www.salon.com/2019/12/31/tulsi-gabbard-impeachment-increased-the-likelihood-that-donald-trump-will-remain-the-president/ (access January 16, 2020).

Russonello, Giovanni, "Scramble for Name Recognition Deep Inside the Margin of Error," The New York Times, October 5, 2019, A10.

Saul, Stephanie, "Tulsi Gabbard Says Kamala Harris Should Apologize for Record as Prosecutor," The New York Times, July 31, 2019, https://www.nytimes.com/2019/07/31/us/politics/kamala-harris-prisoners-tulsi-gabbard.html (accessed October 29, 2019).

Schnall, Marianne, *What Will It Take to Make a Woman President?* (Berkeley: Seal Press, 2013).

Schneider, Monica C. and Bos, A.L. (2014), Measuring Stereotypes of Female Politicians. *Political Psychology*, 35: 245–266. doi:10.1111/pops.12040.

Scott, Eugene, "Why Some African Americans are Questioning Kamala Harris's Blackness," *The Washington Post*, June 28, 2019, https://www.washingtonpost.com/politics/2019/02/14/why-some-african-americans-are-questioning-kamala-harriss-blackness/ (accessed April 8, 2020).

Shapiro, Walter, "Who's Wearing the Pantsuit Now?" *Elle*, July 25, 2009, https://web.archive.org/web/20110307015848/http://www.elle.com/Life-Love/Society-Career-Power/Kirsten-Gillibrand (accessed October 4, 2019).

Spencer, Jim. "Minnesota Sen. Amy Klobuchar details husband's ordeal with COVID-19," *Star Tribune*, March 29, 2020. https://www.startribune.com/minnesota-sen-amy-klobuchar-s-ordeal-with-husband-s-covid-19/569190792/.

Stevens, Matt, "Read Kamala Harris's Vice President-Elect Acceptance Speech," *The New York Times*, November 8, 2020, https://www.nytimes.com/article/watch-kamala-harris-speech-video-transcript.html (accessed November 6, 2020.

Stewart, Patrick A., *Debatable Humor: Laughing Matters on the 2008 Presidential Primary Campaign* (Lexington Books, Lanham, MD: 2012).

Summers, Juana, "Howard University Shaped Kamala Harris' Path to Political Heights," NPR, August 19, 2020. https://www.npr.org/2020/08/19/903716274/howard-university-shaped-kamala-harris-path-to-political-heights (accessed August 25, 2020).

Tankersley, Jim and Ben Casselman, "Trade War and Axes: Where Rivals May Hit Trump on the Economy," *The New York Times*, August 2, 2019, A17.

Ten Presidential Candidates Featured; Gabbard Not Invited," The Daily Wire, December 24, 2019. https://www.dailywire.com/news/dnc-promotes-unity-in-new -ad-with-10-presidential-candidates-gabbards-not-invited (accessed January 30, 2020).

Thomsen, Jacqueline, "Donald Trump: Don't Obsess Over My Genes," *The Hill*, July 5, 2018, https://thehill.com/homenews/senate/395736-warren-fires-back-at -trump-dont-obsess-over-my-genes (accessed June 11, 2020).

Traister, Rebecca, *Good and Mad: The Revolutionary Power of Women's Anger* (New York: Simon and Schuster, 2018), 4.

Wakabayashi, Daisuke, "Gabbard Sues Google, Saying It Stifled Her Speech," *The New York Times*, July 16, 2019, B3.

Warren, Elizabeth and Amelia Warren Tyagi, *All Your Worth: The Ultimate Lifetime Money Plan* (New York: Simon and Schuster, 2005), 6.

Warren, Elizabeth, *This Fight Is Our Fight* (New York: Henry Holt, 2017).

Wegmann, Phillip, "Minnesota Nice Gets Nasty," *RealClear Politics*, February 20, 2020, https://www.realclearpolitics.com/articles/2020/02/20/minnesota_nice_gets _nasty_klobuchar_snaps_at_buttigieg__142446.html (Accessed September 11, 2020).

Williamson, Marianne, *A Politics of Love* (New York: Harper One, 2019).

Williamson, Marianne, *The Age of Miracles* (New York: Hay House, 2008).

Winfrey, Kelly L. Winfrey and James M. Schnoebelen, "Running as a Woman (or Man): A Review of Research on Political Communicators and Gender Stereotypes." *Review of Communication Research*, 7, 2019, 109–138, doi: 10.12840/ISSN.2255- 4165.020.

Witt, Linda, Karen M. Paget and Glenna Matthews, *Running as a Woman: Gender and Power in American Politics* (New York: The Dree Press, 1994), 106.

Zraick, Katherine, "Amy Klobuchar Goes After Elizabeth Warren," *The New York Times*, October 16, 2019. https://www.nytimes.com/2019/10/15/us/politics/amy -klobuchar-elizabeth-warren-debate.html (accessed June 11, 2020).

Index

About the Author

Nichola D. Gutgold is professor of communication arts and sciences at Penn State Lehigh Valley. She is inspired to amplify the voices of women who are often unheard.